CREWING
TO
WIN

SAIL
TO WIN

*Dedicated to my Mum and Dad, thank you for getting me going;
and Han and Joe for all we achieved together.*

*And while I have your attention, can I encourage us all as a sailing
community to do as much as we can to eliminate the use and disposal of
plastic into our fantastic sporting arena. As sailors we are on the front
line, so go over your boat and figure out how you could use less or no PVC
tape, tidy up around your boat space at regattas, and remember to bring
and use reusable water bottles. This is the 11th hour, we have to do better.
Thank you x*

CREWING
TO
WIN

How to be the best crew & a great team

Saskia Clark, MBE

With contributions from
Rob Henderson & Emma McEwen

FERNHURST
BOOKS

Copyright © 2019 Fernhurst Books Limited
First published in 2019 by Fernhurst Books Limited

The Windmill, Mill Lane, Harbury, Leamington Spa, Warwickshire. CV33 9HP, UK
Tel: +44 (0) 1926 337488 | www.fernhurstbooks.com

All rights reserved. No part of this publication may be reproduced, stored in a retrieval system or transmitted, in any form or by any means, electronic, mechanical, photocopying, recording, scanning or otherwise, except under the terms of the Copyright, Designs and Patents Act 1988 or under the terms of a licence issued by The Copyright Licensing Agency Ltd, Saffron House, 6-10 Kirby Street, London EC1N 8TS, UK, without the permission in writing of the Publisher.

Designations used by companies to distinguish their products are often claimed as trademarks. All brand names and product names used in this book are trade names, service marks, trademarks or registered trademarks of their respective owners. The Publisher is not associated with any product or vendor mentioned in this book.

A catalogue record for this book is available from the British Library
ISBN 978-1-912177-24-0

The author and publisher would like to express their considerable thanks to Flora Stewart for helming the 470 in the Weymouth photoshoot, Tim Hore for taking the photographs, the Andrew Simpson Sailing Foundation for providing the RIB and Ian Macwhinnie for driving it.

We would also like to thank Emma and Luke McEwen, Emma Porteous and Tristan Jaques for sailing in the asymmetric photoshoot, Royal Lymington Yacht Club for providing the RIB and Andrew Eady for driving it.

Front cover photograph © Nick Dempsey
Back cover photograph © Thom Touw: Thom Touw Sailing Photography: www.thomtouw.com

All other photographs by Tim Hore © Fernhurst Books Limited
Except: © Thom Touw: p5, 11, 14, 15 (right), 46, 91, 103, 111, 115, 118, 119, 120, 123
© Sportography.tv: p6 (top), 17 (bottom), 33
© Tom Olin: p6 (bottom)
© Jeremy Atkins: p15 (left), 30-32, 35, 42-45, 52-57, 59 (right), 77-87, 89 (bottom)
© Alan Roberts: p17 (top)
© Andy Rice: p58
© Peter Aitken: p75
© Paul Moreau: p51, 101, 102, 110
© Andy Penman: p100

Illustrated by Maggie Nelson & Daniel Stephen
Designed by Daniel Stephen
Printed in Poland by Opolgraf

SASKIA CLARK

GOLD MEDAL & WORLD CHAMPIONSHIP WINNING CREW

Saskia Clark won the 470 gold medal at the Rio Olympics, 2016, sailing with Hannah Mills. This was the culmination of an amazing crewing career which saw her attend 3 Olympic Games, coming sixth in 2008 and getting silver in London 2012 – heart-wrenchingly close to claiming gold.

In the 470 World Championships, Saskia won medals an amazing 6 times over a 10-year period, claiming gold, with Hannah, in 2012.

But is wasn't always like this, Saskia's first experience of sailing was in an Optimist at Dabchicks Sailing Club, aged 8 – she hated it! But her journey shows that, with hard work and determination, and an undoubted natural skill, you can aim for the top and get there!

With Hannah, Saskia was voted World Female Sailor of the Year in 2016 and was appointed an MBE in 2017.

In this book, Saskia shows any crew how they can improve their game, whether they are wanting to win the club race occasionally, be competitive at the national championships or even perform on the international stage.

Olympic Games – Women's 470
- Gold medal, Rio 2016
- Silver medal, London 2012
- 6th place, Beijing 2008

World Championships – Women's 470
- Silver medal, Haifa 2015
- Bronze medal, Santander 2014
- Gold medal, Barcelona 2012
- Silver medal, Perth 2011
- Bronze medal, Cascais 2007
- Silver medal, San Francisco 2005

Other Sailing Titles
- Laser Radial Youth European Champion, 1996
- Optimist Girl's National Champion, 1993

© Thom Touw

OTHER CONTRIBUTORS

Rob Henderson

Having learned to sail with his father in the family Firefly and National 12, Rob went on to the Cadet class and then a Laser. He was a competitive sailor; however, it was not until he left school and went to university that he became fascinated by the intricacies and achievability of sailing quickly. This was largely due to the infectious enthusiasm and confidence of his family and contemporaries.

After spending many seasons deliberating with and learning from sailors such as Will Henderson, Alan Roberts, Jack Holden, Rob Gullan, Frances Peters, Christian Birrell and, most recently, Maria Stanley (2018 Amateur Sailor of the Year), the results started to show with a variety of helms (in brackets):

- RS200 End of Season Champions (Rob Gullan) 2016
- RS200 National Circuit Champions (Maria Stanley) 2017
- RS200 Inland Champions (Maria Stanley) 2017
- 5th at Endeavour Trophy (Christian Birrell) 2017
- RS200 National Tour Champions (Maria Stanley) 2018
- RS200 National Champions (Maria Stanley) 2018

Rob's contributions in this book are in a blue typeface.

Emma McEwen

After a background helming in Toppers and 420s, Emma started crewing whilst team racing at university. Moving on to asymmetric trapezing, she crewed Laser 4000s for four years before taking a five-year sabbatical to sail a cruising boat around the world. She now competes in an RS800 with her husband Luke.

Emma's major crewing achievements are:
- RS800 National Champions, Hayling Island 2016
- RS800 European Champions, Lake Garda 2016
- RS800 European Champions, Medemblik 2017
- RS800 European Champions, Carnac 2018

Emma's contributions in this book are in a green typeface.

CONTENTS

FOREWORD

In all my Olympic sailing career I have sailed as a team – I could have said in a two-person boat, but it is sailing as a team that makes it more than two individual people sailing together. In the preparations for London 2012 I was lucky enough to team up with Saskia Clark who, at that time, had experienced an Olympic Games and medalled at two 470 World Championships.

Sas and I gelled almost instantly, on and off the water. We had similar values, work ethics and of course – goals! In our London 2012 campaign, Sas's experience was a great help to me in so many areas, but most of all – what it means to be a team. In only 18 months together, we qualified for London 2012 and won a silver medal. However, having initially said she would retire, we felt we had more to give and that we could become an even better team for Rio 2016 with a full cycle to prepare. Sas never stopped searching for what being the best crew she could be looked like and we continued learning as a team right up until the last race at Rio.

We had some amazing successes – particularly our gold medal at Rio 2016 – and some fairly tough times, one of which, people might be surprised to hear, was narrowly missing gold at London 2012. To be voted World Sailor of the Year in 2016, jointly with Sas, crowned a fantastic partnership.

In this brilliant book Sas shares her experience of what it takes to be the best crew and make a great team. Any crew, or indeed helm of a two-person boat, would benefit from reading it. Individual skills are covered – like hiking and trapezing, tacking and gybing, hoisting and lowering the spinnaker – and so are the team skills: dividing the roles in the boat both outside competition, pre-start and on each leg of the course. Sas is not prescriptive – she explains how we broke down the roles but is also aware that each team should work to their own strengths and weaknesses and find the best fit.

Reading this book will improve your skills as a crew and make you a better team, whether you are just sailing at your local sailing club or competing internationally at the top of your fleet – I whole-heartedly recommend it.

I also thank Sas for being a great crew but, more importantly, a great team-mate and friend. I'm so proud of all you've achieved with this book.

Hannah Mills
Olympic gold & silver medallist (470), World Champion gold, silver & bronze medallist (470), World Champion (420 and Optimist)

© Thom Touw

INTRODUCTION

MILLS
CLARK

GBR

GBR GBR

PART 1

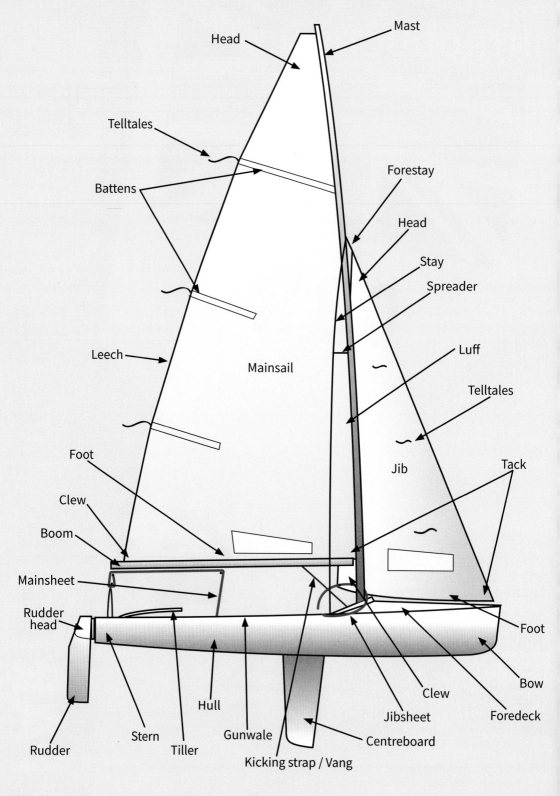

Mast

Head

Telltales

Forestay

Battens

Head

Stay

Spreader

Leech

Luff

Mainsail

Telltales

Foot

Jib

Tack

Clew

Boom

Mainsheet

Rudder head

Foot

Bow

Clew

Jibsheet

Foredeck

Hull

Rudder

Stern

Tiller

Gunwale

Centreboard

Kicking strap / Vang

Hello and welcome to my book!

How we best work as a team will never be the same as another partnership: we will come to the boat with different experiences, varying strengths and weakness, and practical stuff such as different weight combinations and heights will all alter the best way to do things.

This book is not designed to be read in one go and then go off and become a sailor. Get sailing, enjoy what you are doing and come back to this if you get stuck on processes and need a few ideas to break through.

If a section is on a green background that topic is aimed at beginners. There is also a glossary at the back to help describe sailing terms you might not know. Opposite there is a diagram of a boat, just so that you know what I am referring to in the book. There are other diagrams as appropriate in the book.

Saskia Clark

Get sailing and enjoy what you're doing!

CHAPTER 2
Getting Started

Being A Crew

Crewing is often a simple way to get into sailing: you can put a notice on your local sailing club's board or Facebook page advertising your keenness and from there could easily get some crewing time on yachts or a dinghy.

I think it's for this reason that crewing is often considered to be not as important as the helming role: because you can just jump in and go.

In the early days of your crewing career this might be the case but if you want to form a world-beating team, contribute equally to the speed, decision making and outcome of your racing, or simply understand better what is going on, then hopefully this book will be useful to you.

Hannah and I became a world-beating team
© Thom Touw

Choosing A Boat

The choice of boats is huge.

If you are new to sailing, it's likely that you will go along with whatever you get invited to sail on – and that is a great way to get experience in different types of boats and sailing with different people.

If you are thinking about buying a boat, get down to your local club and see what kind of racing is happening, whether it is one design or handicap and join in with a similar size or type of boat. Other important considerations are:

- How much you want to be pushed physically (will it be hard work for you to sail this class?)
- How much time you have to invest in upkeep (a wooden boat takes a lot of care and attention, while a glass fibre boat is less work, but some types of glass fibre boats still require quite a bit of maintenance)

Forming A Team

I realise that a blank canvas to build your team is unlikely, but a few things to consider when thinking about what and who you would want to sail with.

Weight, Height & Physicality
These will be deciding factors on the boat that you will be most suited too.

If you are tall, trapezing would be a great avenue for you because of your superior leverage; if you're shorter, it will present a challenge in the windier conditions.

If you are heavier than optimum for your choice of boat, ideally you would team up with a small helm to stay competitive against others and likewise, if you are on the smaller side for a crew, a bigger helm would help.

Some boats, like the RS800 are weight-equalised so that everyone is equally competitive in all wind ranges, regardless of size and weight. The RS800 is both weight and righting-moment equalised with light-weight teams carrying extra lead and short teams on wider rack settings.

Racing and sailing can be as physical as you want to make it, but talk to other sailors about the challenges the boats they sail bring and think about whether that is something you could embrace and enjoy.

Make sure your goals are compatible: Hannah and I wanted to win, but also had fun! © Thom Touw

Crewing on an asymmetric boat can be a physical work-out

Your Goals As A Sailor

It's important that your goals align well within your team. If one of you is all about the social and fun and the other is interested in winning titles it will be hard to create a fulfilling atmosphere. But importantly those categories are not mutually exclusive to each other and often having fun is one of the keys to success, but it is worth having those conversations early on to avoid arguments.

Your Skills

There might be the option to form a team with sailors from a variety of different backgrounds (e.g. 2 helms from single-handers, 2 crews with one moving to a helming role). Whatever your previous experience, it won't prevent or make you less likely to become a great team in the future but, when you are thinking about starting a new partnership, it's a good time for a bit of self-reflection: question what your existing skills are and consider potential team-mates that would complement them. It's definitely worth canvassing opinion on this as we all tend to have blindspots in how we view ourselves.

Your Crewing Role

If you are new to sailing, as soon as you have a basic understanding of what is going on in the boat, it is important to take ownership of the roles that are appropriate, if you want to be more than just a passenger.

In this book, each chapter deals with what the crew's roles have been in my experience, but I think it's important to realise that everyone will bring their own skills to the boat, so things might work out differently in your team.

CHAPTER 3

A Day On The Water

What To Wear

If you are just giving sailing a go then just wear something that you are happy to get wet in, ideally quick drying and take some kind of wind / waterproof jacket if you have it, as it will always be colder on the water than you are expecting. Any kind of trainers will be fine.

If you are committed to spending some money, then my vote would be for a good fitting wetsuit with quality neoprene, so it is nice and flexible. I prefer wearing a long john wetsuit and layering up on thermals as it gets cold, rather than a steamer, to keep mobility in my shoulders and elbows.

Boots with a good grip but flexible sole are a vital bit of crewing equipment. Some people pull off bare feet whilst crewing, but stubbing your toe is one of the most painful experiences known to humans, so it's not something for me. Also, there is the uncomfortable bit of launching in bare feet.

My boots are flexible, but with good grip

For me, gloves are a must when going out sailing, except if it is very light winds. I use full-finger gloves except for thumb and index finger, so that you can do fiddly knots and split rings. It's important that the gloves are not so thick that you lose grip.

I use full-finger gloves except for the thumb and index finger

In the summer, many like to wear a baseball hat to keep the sun and spray out their eyes. In the winter, a woolly hat is an affordable way to stay comfortable in cold weather. Do ensure there is somewhere to put it during a race if things heat up. This can be a pouch on the boat somewhere or it can just be tucked under a buoyancy aid.

Hiking

Here and elsewhere in this book, I have asked Rob Henderson to give advice on hiking boats specifically.

Dressed in 'hot and light' mode (right)

For my summer wetsuit, I prefer the use of 'hiker' or 'long-john' style wetsuits. My current wetsuit covers the legs and hooks over the shoulders, while leaving the arms entirely free. This basic set-up gives me full protection throughout the wind range, articulation and the ability to accessorise based on temperature, precipitation and wind conditions.

In the winter I like to wear a drysuit. Although bulkier and rather more expensive, I think that comfort, warmth and being dry are the priorities.

The other main consideration is footwear. Footwear is often an afterthought, with some choosing to forgo it entirely and, contrary to their tough persona, to their detriment. Saskia's advice about footwear also applies to hiking dinghies, however it is also important for boots to grip the toestraps, distribute the load across the foot comfortably and strike the right balance between rigid support and ergonomics. In an RS200, I opt for an all-round boot that is light and flexible enough for me to move around smoothly and be

The same kit with an additional layer underneath and a spray top in more breeze so I stay warm and dry

comfortable when fully squatted, but also ensures that I can lock into an effective hiking position for an extended period of time.

Having said this, I do have a heftier pair of boots either for use in the winter for extra warmth and / or at clubs where the launching area is rough or requires good grip underfoot. Under these circumstances, the pain is not worth it. If you can't feel your feet because they are cold then you are in trouble, regardless of how much 'feel' the boot claims to give.

Trapezing

For trapeze crews, a comfortable harness will take some finding: different models will offer

I wear a long john wetsuit with thermals and a front lace up harness

different levels of support across your back and shoulders, and finding the right shape can really help manage any back problems you may have. I am always looking to get locked in to the seat of my harness so prefer the lace up fronts; if you are using kinetics (pumping and bouncing), it means that more energy transfers up the wire to the mast rather than getting lost in a baggy harness. I use a lightweight, flexible nappy harness in light winds, for maximum manoeuvrability.

It's a great idea to try them on and put them under load, so try to rig up some kind of 'trapeze wire' so you can actually feel how they fit, where they are supporting you and where you might want more support. Remember to crouch into a ball to replicate light wind, in-the-boat sailing.

Food, Drink & Sunscreen

I think that, maybe, being hungry is more miserable than being cold, so good snacks are vital to an enjoyable day on the water! There are whole books written about sports nutrition and food for performance, so I'll leave that up to them. Personally, having something I really like, so I can eat it quickly and often enough to maintain a positive energy balance is more important than the detail of the nutritional value.

Again, drinking enough when racing is hard, so make sure it's something you actually like. If you are trying to build or maintain a weight, it's important to consider how many calories you are getting through your drink and whether here is a good opportunity to add or take away calories.

Always have something ready for the tow / sail in or on shore to eat. You'll be surprised how much energy 3 races in cold conditions uses and it's hard to eat enough in the gap between races. If you've got a championship week, this WILL make a difference as the week goes on.

And finally, it is so easy to forget sunscreen, but we know that the water reflects the sun and so a day on the water is a day exposed to the sun. Build applying sunscreen into your routine, so you don't forget it.

PART 2

SKILLS

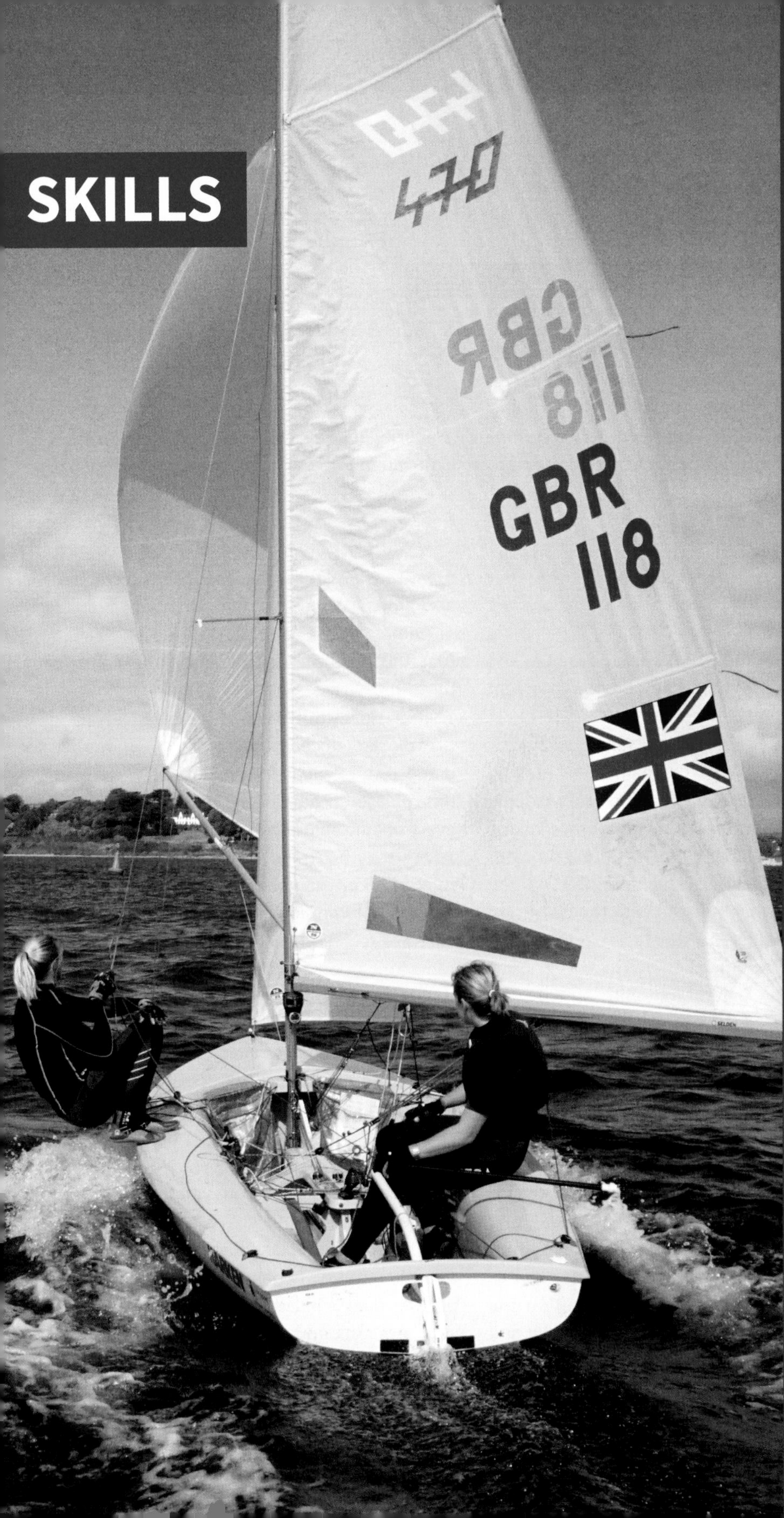

CHAPTER 4

Hiking Technique

Since most of my recent experience is in a symmetric trapezing dinghy, I've asked top hiking crew, Rob Henderson, to contribute this chapter. You can read on p6 about Rob's achievements and why what he says is worth reading!

Starting Out

Hiking is essentially very simple: you are maximising your leverage on the hull / rig by hooking your feet under the toestrap and extending the suitable amount of weight overboard.

If you are new to hiking, go sailing with your helm and have a play. The main aim being to instil your confidence and feel for it. Try sailing in breeze that is strong enough to make hiking necessary, but light enough for you and your partner to sail safely without doing so. As you sail, try to familiarise yourself with the sensation of hiking while trimming sheets, looking around and talking to the helm.

Once you are comfortable with straight-line sailing and hiking, you can look at tacking and becoming happy with hooking your feet into the toestraps after the tack instinctively rather than cognitively.

Advanced Techniques

You will quickly master the basics of hiking and realise that, as soon as conditions approach those in which the rig is 'powered up' and requires righting moment beyond the just sitting on the gunwale, the crew's ability to hike effectively and for longer than their competitors is one of the greatest weapons available on a hiking dinghy.

As a relatively big crew in the RS200, it took many seasons for me to refine my hiking technique and fitness. When I started out, I weighed 80kgs, did not consider toestrap position and assumed that those out-hiking me just had higher pain thresholds, leg strength and cardiovascular ability... How wrong I was.

The art of effective hiking requires some practice, refinement and enjoyment. When reading this, please do bear in mind that everybody and every boat is built differently and so, although my advice may be useful, it is not the hard and fast rulebook. For example, the two boats I sail at the moment (Merlin Rocket and RS200) require quite different techniques but are underpinned by the same fundamental principles.

Some crews like to cross their legs or drop their bottom right down outside the gunwale with their chests up against their knees. Although these techniques might feel comfortable for a while, they leave you prone to injury and do not do the boat's speed as much good as hiking with good technique.

If your legs are crossed, you are straining the ligaments across your knees and distorting your back. Furthermore, if a quick movement forward or aft is required (when the boat begins or stops planing downwind or in waves upwind), having your legs crossed is not a dynamic position from which to begin.

'Drop hiking' can give the crew the feeling that

they are hiking effectively, however you would be more useful perched on the side deck and applying a slight lean overboard, such is the extent of your centre of gravity in this position. Not only are you likely to drag your backside in the water when the boat is flat and jerk the boat when it comes to a lull or tack, you are putting undue strain on your knees and shins. As with crossing your legs, you are little stuck when you are hooked over the side deck should your weight need to be shifted.

In lighter winds, the crew may not sit on the side deck all day long, and so your movements will need to be refined, smooth and your static positions sustainable. Any movements that are not smooth tend to jerk not only the wind out of the sails, but the helm's concentration.

You are working dynamically from a crouched position in the cockpit (bilges!) to your hiking position and any range in between. Work with your helm to establish their preferred movements around the boat and where your body should be in various conditions.

In addition, a hiking crew has greater influence over fore / aft movements than a crew on a trapeze wire. When sailing with Frances and Maria, I was very much the heavier member of the team and so my movements over the waves and through the puffs both upwind and downwind were critical.

Things To Make Life Easier

As well as working on your fitness, you can set your boat up to enable you to hike better and for longer.

Toestraps

If they are too tight, your 'maximum extension' position is limited, and / or you will be in the helm's eyeline. If they are too loose, then you will be out of control, your legs will be taking all of the strain (which is unsustainable) and / or your backside will trail in the water.

Leg length and boat shape are the two main factors when setting up your toestraps.

Compared to most RS200 crews, I am relatively tall and therefore find the standard toestrap set-up uncomfortable. Normally, the crew's toestraps are anchored underneath the thwart on the aft end and under the jib cleats forward. I like to have the forward ends anchored to the hog in the middle of the boat (about a foot further inboard!) and the toestraps relatively tight. This gives me the ability to get my centre of gravity a good distance outboard in a sustainable position – knees slightly bent, feet only slightly strained to maintain the hook on the strap and my legs contacting the deck about ¾ of the way up my hamstrings.

On a Merlin or RS400, on the other hand, the cockpits are relatively deep, wide and generously decked, so it can be nice to have the toestraps further outboard and looser.

Using shock cord to high points on the boat will lift the toestrap off the floor of the boat so that you can get your feet underneath without hindrance.

Sheets

Saskia's advice regarding jib cleat position and angle (p29) is equally applicable in hiking dinghies. However, do also make sure that the sheets themselves are long enough for you to go about your crewing functions as easily while you are hiking as when you are crouched in the cockpit.

On asymmetric boats, I like to have the kite sheets long enough for me to trim from the back of the boat in windy weather without the windward (lazy) sheet being pulled at all (when this happens, the clew of the sail gets pulled inboard and forward, which is detrimental to trim). The jibsheets should be long enough to be within arm's reach in this position.

Jib and kite sheets on asymmetric dinghies tend to be continuous for good reason.

Having said all this, sheets that are too long can get tangled. It is worth erring on the long side to start with and cutting sheets down afterwards (you cannot grow rope)!

CHAPTER 5

Trapezing Technique

Starting Out

When starting out trapezing remember that pretty much the worst that can happen is that you get wet.

Any anxiety you have about trapezing will quickly go, so let's get started and out on the wire!

- Trim your jib to the correct place.
- Pull your hook height so you will just skim the deck when attached and have the jibsheet in your back hand.
- Clip on and relax in your harness and feel that the trapeze wire is taking your weight.
- As the wind increases, and the boat begins to tip, use your back leg on the floor / centreboard case to push yourself out over the side until your front leg finds it's footing on the gunwale. Use your hands to steady yourself on the gunwale or shroud if needed.
- As the wind increases further, straighten your front leg until your back foot can join your front foot on the gunwale.
- If you've lost your jibsheet in the process, crouch down and get it or get your helm to pass it out to you.

Clip on

Sit with the trapeze taking your weight

Bend your front leg

Push out with your back leg

Push out with your front leg

So both feet are on the gunwale

Push yourself out

Straightening your front leg first

Until both legs are straight

Through the whole process, keep your weight pressed into your harness and through the wire so there is then never any slack and you don't come unclipped.

Have your feet whatever distance apart feels comfortable for balance. As you gain confidence, move your feet closer together.

Initially you will probably have your feet apart for balance

But, as you grow more confident, you can move your feet closer together

If there is enough wind, lean back in your harness, so you can feel the shoulder straps tension, take your hands away from the cleats and handles. Have the harness shoulder straps tight enough so they support your back and stop you over-arching. As you do more hours, you'll notice your back and abdominals getting stronger.

Fully out on the wire

Coming in is simply the reverse:
- Bend your back leg.
- Slide into the boat until your back leg hits the centreboard case.
- Unweight your front leg and slide in fully.

From straight legs

Begin bending your legs

Carry on bending your legs

Until your back leg is in

Followed by your front leg

Move towards sitting on the side deck

You will move through this phase very quickly.

Advanced Technique

You will quickly become confident on the wire. As you get more confident, and gain some sailing-specific strength, your technique will become more advanced.

- With your front hand, hold on to your handle without hooking on to the wire and take your body weight through your arm. Jibsheet in your back hand.
- Swing out on to the side using the same technique as before.
- Clip on to the trapeze hook when you are out there.

Hold the handle and push out

Without hooking on

Grab the hook when you are out there

Clip on

Let go of the handle

And go fully out

Before you do this, try to have your trapeze hook in about the right place for the wind speed, otherwise you could end up too low, and in the water, or too high.

As the wind increases the power, speed and aggression that you do this movement will to.

In lighter winds there are 2 options:

1. Continue doing the original method, as you may sometimes be trapezing off the centreboard case, continually having your weight committed into the harness will keep the rig steady, smooth and fast.
2. Alternatively, hike the boat down in this wind speed to avoid disrupting the rig by hooking on and off continually.

Hiking without the trapeze

Trapezing off the centreboard from behind

Trapezing off the centreboard from leeward

Your first main job as a crew is keeping the boat flat so, sailing in a straight line, the aim is to keep a consistent heel angle. This is not always horizontal; the boat might prefer sitting with 10 degrees of heel and this will change through the wind and wave range. Through some tuning decide with your team-mate what the best angle of heel is and then work on maintaining that. This will be a continually moving feast and, because the helm has the tiller, they are normally much more sensitive to it than you will be as a crew. A big part of your upwind speed will be getting this right and continually monitoring it.

As the wind increases, lean back and commit your shoulders into your harness. As it decreases bend your legs. Bending your legs, rather than lifting your shoulders up is a smoother transition of less leverage on the wire: lifting your shoulders up can disrupt the rig.

Try to never get to the point where you are crouched awkwardly on the gunwale, especially if your bottom is lower than your feet. If the wind decreases further from this point it is a really awkward and clumsy move to get your legs out from underneath you and will shake the wind from the rig. Always bring your back leg in before this happens.

As the wind decreases, bend your legs so you can swing into the boat easily

Avoid crouching awkwardly on the gunwale with your bottom lower than your feet

All your movements send a jolt up the trapeze wire to the mast and this unsettles the airflow over the sail. For optimum speed, try to keep all your movements smooth: bending your legs rather than touching the trapeze adjuster can really help this.

Things To Make Life Easier

Getting the right jib and kite sheet length is really important to making your life easier. Long enough so you can do all your jobs, but not overlong so they just get tied into a knot and caught on everything.

Handle Height

As well as the trapeze adjustment system, which is likely to be limited in the class rules of your boat as to how many cleats and blocks you are allowed, you can include another rope system (above the handle) to move the handle height depending on wind strength.

Trapeze height adjustment below the handle

Additional trapeze height adjustment above the handle – set high

Ideally set your average trapezing position for the conditions so that you will be straight-leg trapezing most of the time. Hopefully that's achievable by raising or lowering the gross adjustment of your trapeze wire length so that your trapeze hook adjustment system gives you enough travel to allow for lulls and gusts.

Shock Cord

Some shock cord (bungee) in the trapeze system from the top cleat down to the trapeze hoop is also really useful. This keeps the trapeze system tidy and taught so, when it's windy and the trapeze hook is max low, it is not swinging around into your face and is in the right place on the exit of a tack.

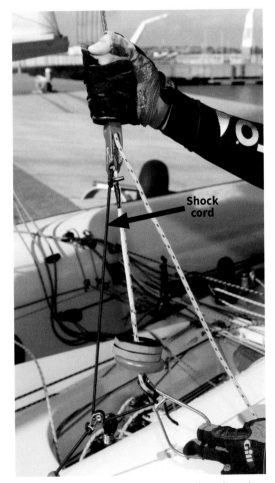

Shock cord

Shock cord to keep the trapeze system tidy and taught

Jib Cleat Height

If you are finding that your jibsheet is hard to get in the cleat, it's possible that the cleat is too low. Alternatively, if it's hard to get your sheet out of the cleat, they could be too high. You can alter the jib cleat height, in terms of fore and aft position and height up from the floor. Ideally you want your sheet to slide nicely into the cleat jaws whilst in your 'average' crewing position.

If the cleat is too low the sheet will pop out when you are not expecting it as you are not using enough of the cleat's jaws. If the cleat is too high the jibsheet will be wedged in and it is too hard to get out of the cleat. Obviously, this is affected by what height you are trapezing or hiking at so it will be a compromise.

To make a cleat or cleat and block higher, either use the special angled wedges from the manufacturer, or simply cut out some chopping board pieces, which support the whole of the cleat and block shape, to mount it all on top of. If you still have a problem, check where your block feeds the sheet into your cleat – that might need some alteration to find the sweet spot.

Changing the fore and aft position is harder but possible. If you always have to reach awkwardly either forward or back to get your jibsheet in the cleat it could be worth moving it. Have a think about how you cross the boat through the tack and whether moving them would make it easier for you. There needs to be some structural integrity to the deck at the new mounting place. Simply bolting them to any bit of the side deck will not be strong enough, so get someone who knows what they are doing to advise you.

Make sure your jibsheet cleat is in the right position

Asymmetric Trapezing

For advice on asymmetric / skiff trapezing, I am grateful to Emma McEwen for contributing this section.

If you are trapeze crewing an asymmetric dinghy then all the principles described by Saskia for symmetric trapeze dinghies remain the same; upwind, move smoothly in and out on the wire to keep the required angle of balance and adjust your trapeze handle height to be most ergonomic.

You will find the boat more stable in stronger winds when you trapeze low with your shoulders back to keep your weight low. In moderate, gusty conditions where the lulls mean that you need to bend your knees quickly to reduce your leverage, you will find it easier to trapeze higher to ensure that you can clear the rack / gunwale with your bottom as your range of movement may need to go from fully flat wiring to inside the boat very rapidly to avoid pulling the boat in to windward if you hit the water.

The trim of the boat is also very important with a skiff dinghy, so practise moving forward and aft along the gunwale (or rack tube) so you become confident with your footwork and you and your helm can learn where best to position weight in different conditions to get the best speed and reduce the risk of pitchpoling (when your weight is too far forward).

Upwind you will, at some point in the wind range, need to transition from trapezing behind the shrouds (out on the rack), to trapezing off the foredeck forward of the shrouds. In very light conditions you will need to sit, squat or kneel on the foredeck to have your weight far enough forward to get the transom out the water to eliminate its drag.

The main difference in trapezing style for a skiff is that, when the shape of the boat is a flat dish with wide racks, you will need to stand up when you are in the boat during manoeuvres and pre-start and transitioning to the wire should ideally not involve sitting down. The exact footwork will vary depending on your height (leg length) and how wide the boat is that you sail. This is how I move in a RS800 on maximum rack width:

Trapezing behind the shrouds   *Moving forwards*   *Trapezing in front of the shrouds*

To go out on the wire:

- From standing (wide stance for stability), facing forward in the boat, turn to face the edge of the boat.
- Step with your leeward foot on to the inner edge of the gunwale while reaching out ahead of you to pick up the trapeze handle with one hand (sheet in the other).
- Now step with other foot out on to edge of the rack. Keep tension on the trapeze wire by pushing it straight out ahead of you to steady your balance.
- Rotate on your outer foot to turn your body to face into the boat while bringing your other foot out on to the rack too (now your aft foot).
- Drop back and push off so you are hanging off one arm holding the trapeze handle, so your body is held straight and tall. Keeping your trapeze handle arm straight will require less strength than if your arm is bent.
- Now raise your hips up and, with your sheet hand, bring the trapeze loop to your harness to clip on.
- Adjust the height of the trapeze if you need to, but then remove both hands from the trapeze handle and lie back, shoulders down.

From standing in a wide stance

Turn, step with your leeward foot and reach for the trapeze handle

Step onto the edge of the rack, keeping tension in the trapeze wire

Turn your body to face in to the boat

Stand on the rack

Drop back and push off

Clip on

Extend your body

Until fully out

To come in:

- If wiring low, raise your height a little with the adjuster.
- Keep your body straight but reach up with your forward hand to the handle.
- Now bend your knees a little to enable you to dynamically stand up on the rack.
- As you come to standing, the trapeze should fall off your hook but knock it down with your aft (sheet) hand if it hasn't.
- Keep momentum by pushing the trapeze handle out behind you as you step into the boat with your aft foot on to the inner gunwale.
- Your forward foot steps into the bottom of the boat, your aft foot goes across to the far side and you are back to wide stance forward facing standing position again.

From fully out on the trapeze

Reach for the handle & bend your knees

Come in further

Stand up on the rack

Move into the boat

Return to the wide stance in the centre of the boat

If you are sailing a boat with the option to put the wires forward or aft of the shrouds, then consider the wind condition forecast for the day and set aft if windy and forward if light. This will make it easier to wire further aft in windy weather without less forward pull on the wire. In light winds, when wiring off the foredeck, the wire will not snag on the shrouds so much if it is led forward.

Trapezing Downwind

In a fast asymmetric dinghy, the main thrill is that you will be on the wire whilst flying the kite downwind. This is the ultimate high-speed adrenalin rush and maximum exhilaration!

You will feel most stable if you drop down on your wire rather than wiring high – otherwise you will feel like you will fall into the boat if any leeward heel is induced. You will need to move further aft in the boat than upwind and, as you go

aft, your trapeze hook naturally gets higher. You will find you need to let your adjuster out further for downwind compared to upwind trapezing.

The windier the conditions, the further aft you need to move your body. In rough and windy conditions, getting one foot into a footloop as far aft as possible will be most secure. If helm and crew both have one footloop you will need to step your aft leg back over the helm's forward leg once they are locked in their footloop to get into yours. Putting your aft hand gently on the helms knee (if they don't mind!) while you do this can make it feel more stable. Practise getting in and out of the footloop until you can do it confidently without needing to look for the loop; your eyes should always be on the kite.

Getting out on the wire is the same as upwind but you will be holding the kite sheet and trimming the kite actively in the process.

Trapezing downwind with your back foot in the footloop

CHAPTER 6

Tacking

I write from the perspective of a double-handed, single-trapeze boat as that was my speciality. It may at times feel very specific to that type of dinghy. However, I hope the level of detail, as well as Rob's and Emma's contributions, will illustrate the different ways of doing things and the areas to focus on will be a useful tool for all crewing roles as you problem solve your way to getting better.

Basic Tack

Tacking is when the front of the boat goes through head to wind. When you are learning to sail, it is the 'safe' way to change direction as, when the boat is pointing directly into the wind, there is no wind in the sail creating power so it's slower.

On the entry you are on the opposite side of the boat to the sail; as you head into the tack, everything is in the middle at the same point: you, the wind and therefore the boom. On the exit, aim to hit the new side of the boat as the boom hits its new powered-up position.

When you are learning to crew, essentially you want your weight to transfer in harmony with the turning circle of the boat and your helmsperson, to balance out the pressure in the sails.

- Pre-tack pull the slack out of your windward jibsheet.
- Balance your transfer across so the boat stays level without any heel either on the entry or exit.
- Travel though the boat facing forwards or backwards – one will naturally make sense depending on the boat.
- As the jib flaps when the boat is head to wind, uncleat the jib and be ready to pull it in on the new side.
- When the boat has completed its turn, pull in the new jibsheet and balance the boat on the new tack.

The process will vary in speed depending on whether you are tacking beat-to-beat (faster) or reach-to-reach (slower). It will also depend on the wind strength and wave conditions. It's important not to pull the jib in on the new side before the boat has gone through head to wind, as this could push you back to the old direction as the wind in the sail works against the steering. As you are learning, err on the side of changing the jib and side too late rather than early.

Communication

At this first stage it is really important to build up a robust communication method between you and your helmsperson, that will survive any scenario and pressure.

The correct seamanship communication for tacking is for the helmsperson to (jauntily) hail, 'Ready about?'. When the crew replies, 'Ready', the helm says 'Lee-Ho!' as they push the tiller away.

We tend to go for a general 'ready to tack', wait for an answer, and a countdown of '2', '1', 'Go' from the helm with the 'Go' being the point at which the turn starts. The countdown expresses the tempo of the tack. If it's a lightwind tack the '2', '1' will be slow to set the tempo. A fast '2', '1' and it's a fast and snappy tack.

- On the 'ready to tack', pull out any slack in the windward jibsheet.
- On '2', drop the active jibsheet neatly away from your feet and away from where you will

Pull the slack out of the windward jibsheet

Balance the boat as it begins to turn

As the jib begins to back

Release the jibsheet

And pull it in the other side

Sail off on the other tack

be travelling through the boat: this could be behind or in front of you.

- On '1', if you are hiking, free your back foot from the toestrap. If you are trapezing, take your weight in your front hand and knock the trapeze hoop off your harness hook with your back hand.
- On 'Go', the tiller gets pushed away and the tack starts.

Execution

As you are learning and gelling with a new team-mate, be strict with your process. Don't get lazy and miss things out in your preparation or communication. As you get better, parts of the process you can refine, drop or build, but having a repeatable process is the first step in being able to review and change something for the better.

Get your helm to watch your footwork, timing and hand positions (or mount an action camera looking backwards or down from the spreaders). Doing this you will notice things that you don't feel on the water.

Ideally you will be totally ambidextrous, so always able to use your front and back hand / legs / feet for the same thing NOT your left for some things and your right for others.

In the business of a race, especially when you are around other boats, it is a really important skill to disengage from the racing action, bring your concentration internal and execute a great tack without distraction. If you are finding that difficult, it might work to have a cue to make that happen so, when you know a tack is coming, look at the place where you want your back foot to hit on the floor of the boat as you come in. Or, as you drop your jibsheet, look across the boat and sight the bit of jibsheet you are going to put your back hand on to uncleat. Things like this will bring your focus internal to execute.

Roll Tack

As you get better at sailing you will use your body weight to generate power in the sails, which will translate into boatspeed.

As a general rule, if you can pull your mast fast through the air to vertical, but not past it, it will generate forward momentum. Tacking is a great opportunity for this, although you should take care only to get back up to your previous speed rather than increase your speed as a result of the roll tack (which is against the rules).

- On '2', slightly unweight with your hiking or trapezing to get some leeward heel into the boat, which will help steer it into the wind. Ideally the whole process of getting the boat head to wind would be done with minimal rudder movement.
- As the bow hits head to wind, aggressively transfer your weight to the old windward side in one swift movement, to initiate a sharp heel. There are a few things that you can use to lock yourself into the boat and generate a positive connected energy transfer. If you have a toestrap, aggressively hike out on it or grip it with your front hand and hike. I hook my toes under the centreboard case, hike aggressively with my upper body and then use the other side of the centreboard case to pull me back in and help me climb up. If you are in a trapeze boat, you can use the trapeze wire to pull down on to initiate the windward roll, although I found this method hard to build consistency in and it can end up with a bit of an uncontrollable exit.
- Uncleat the jib and gather in on the new side but don't oversheet it.
- Keep that heel on until the boat is nearing its exit angle of the tack.
- As you hit the exit angle, pull the boat down to horizontal and trim in the jib.

All this will be done in harmony with the helm's movements and steering. Things to really focus on are:
- Different wind speeds will want a shorter or

Initiate a roll to leeward to help the boat turn

Roll the boat to windward

Sit on the new windward deck

Move to roll the boat to windward

At head to wind begin to initiate the roll to windward

Uncleat the old jib and start gathering it in on the new side

Cross the boat to the new windward side

Pulling the boat upright and trim the jib

And start sailing normally again

longer backing of the jib: this will be something to develop in conjunction with your helm and what they feel on the steering.

- When you are pulling the boat flat on the exit, NEVER go past horizontal. The idea of the pull flat is to accelerate the wind off the sail, if you over flatten you depower again.

- Newton's 3rd Law: every action has an equal and opposite reaction, which in this context means: it is easy to put power into the windward roll on the tack entry because, as the boat is steering into the wind, it is depowering. Be aware that on the exit of the tack you have to take that roll off when the boat is powering up as wind is filling into the sail. It's not an excuse to go easy but you should know that you can get the boat flat on the exit.

- Be aware of what the wind conditions are doing: if the wind has dropped during the race, say out loud that you need to slow down the tempo and actively put more energy into manoeuvres. Conversely if the wind has built, you need your actions to be more snappy and dynamic.

The roll tack is simpler as a hiking crew or as a trapeze crew when it's lighter as you are off the wire.

Hiking Boat Tack

Saskia has comprehensively covered the basics of manoeuvring the boat as a team and the principles of tacking in a hiking boat, as this is what a 470 is when it is light enough for the crew to not trapeze. There are some subtle differences that will largely come through practice and comparing techniques with those popular at the front of the fleet. For example, many hiking boats do not respond well to an initial leeward heel before a tack. The desired effect is to assist with luffing the boat into the wind and therefore reduce the helm's use of the rudder, however, in some classes with shorter foils, doing so can cause the boat to slip sideways and stall just when you do not want it to.

My tip when it comes to any manoeuvre is that speed is your friend, be it light or windy, so make sure that how the boat is moving comes to mind before a tack. Sometimes, a polite utterance of 'get her moving' from the crew can make the helm delay for a second or two to get the boat back up to speed before the tack. They might not thank you for it, but it can make life a lot easier.

Additionally, many hiking boats do not require a huge amount of roll for an effective roll tack. A Firefly, for example, requires the movement that Saskia describes to initiate the required amount; however, an RS200 only requires a small amount of roll in light airs, preferring instead to glide further to windward in a smooth and a gentle arcing tack.

In medium breeze, the art of synchronisation between helm and crew is most critical. To start with, you must work out as a team how much roll through and correction afterwards is going to be necessary in the given conditions. This is best done by launching in good time before the race and getting a feel for it on the practice beat. Thereafter, the crew can establish how much body movement is needed before the tack and where they need to be after the tack to correct the heel. In these conditions, the exit to the tack is critical. Whether you are inboard, perched on the side deck or hiking out after the tack, it is beneficial to reach this position at the very same time as the helm reaches theirs.

A team that masters this art not only looks great and psyches out competitors but also ensures that the rig is brought upright in one motion. If helm and crew 'hit the new side' at different times, the rig gets jolted (and therefore the wind is knocked from the sail) twice rather than once and it is difficult for both team-mates to feel their way out the tack.

Once I had sailed an RS200 for a few seasons and was happy with how the jib should be sheeted, I actually started to spend the second half of medium wind tacks watching the helm to make sure that I was moving (and stopping!) in unison with them.

In windier conditions, the key is to keep the

boat flat and under control. Just remember that although the few seconds of hiking after a tack may be the most difficult, they are the most important of all. Broadly speaking, hiking boats are slower than trapeze boats and therefore carry less momentum through and are more difficult to get going again after a tack. Maria and I may not always have pulled off the most beautiful looking windy weather tacks, but we made sure that we delivered maximum effort after them to iron them out.

Trapezing Boat Roll Tack

As a trapeze crew, as the breeze builds there might be a small wind bracket where it is easier to come off the wire, keep the wire loaded through your arm but effectively roll tack as if you are hiking.

It gets a little bit trickier as the breeze builds and your regular trapezing position is with straight legs and you are committed to the harness, but it is still a light enough breeze for roll tacking to be a benefit.

In terms of what you are trying to achieve, nothing much changes but it's harder to be consistent in getting the windward heel on in the entry and your agility at which you get across the boat and the power with which you hit the new windward side are key as it will load up quickly.

Practice will make this perfect and aim to build a roll tack that consistently hits 85% of its speed potential rather than one that is boom or bust. Make sure that your body weight stays over your feet so that you can always push up and run across the boat. If your feet get above your body weight it's easy to get left behind.

Wire-To-Wire Tack

When the boat is nearing max power, which is when you are fully committed to the harness, rarely bending your knees and on tip toes to keep the boat flat, it is basically faster to have the boat going flat in one direction and to get it going flat in the other direction as quickly as possible:

- Use the same communication as our other tacks.
- Pre-tack pull the jibsheet tight on the lazy (windward) side.
- On '2', drop the jibsheet into the water behind you and take your body weight into your front arm and knock the trapeze loop out of your harness hook. As much as possible you want to stay at max leverage, so keep your core tight so the heel of the boat doesn't increase.
- The helm will tack as normal.
- Swing into the boat, depending on how high the gunwales are you might sit down or stay standing on your feet. As you do this, with your back hand reach across to the working jib cleat and uncleat the sheet but, importantly, keep the tension of the jib in your arm, whilst your front hand locates and grips the lazy sheet where it is exiting from the windward cleat. This will coincide with the boat being near head to wind.
- As the boat goes through head to wind, let the old jibsheet go and, as you duck the boom and travel across the boat to the new windward side, take the new loaded jibsheet with you, in what will now be your back hand, so you effectively pull it in as you travel across the boat.
- As soon as your head is under the boom, look up to locate where the windward trapeze handle is and grab it with your new front hand, swinging straight out on the new windward side, kicking off the centreboard case or floor of the boat.
- Trim your jibsheet near enough correct, that might mean it slips a bit through your hand as you move out to maximum extension, or you pull it in a bit more with your arm.
- Keep your weight solid in your front arm, the boat might need a little pull down flat.
- Hook on and settle in to the new angle. Get your jibsheet trimmed right.

The speed of this action is totally dependent upon the wind speed and waves. In flat water it will probably be the most consistent and fluid but, with choppy water, parts will slow down and speed up

Wire-To-Wire Tack

From trapezing at maximum leverage, drop the jibsheet behind you

With your weight on your front arm, knock the trapeze hoop from your harness and start to come in as the helm steers into the tack

As you sit on the side deck, locate your back hand on the working jibsheet and have your front hand ready on the jibsheet near your knees

As you go through head to wind, uncleat the old jibsheet and grip the new sheet

Duck for the boom, stand up pulling the jibsheet with you and aim your new front hand to the windward trapeze handle

Spring from the centreboard case or floor straight onto the gunwale

Trim the jib to about right

Clip onto the trapeze and fine tune the jib

Resume trapezing

as the boat hits and gets powered up by the waves. Things to concentrate on are:

- Don't let any power go in the entrance to the tack, keep max leverage as long as possible.
- Get the old jibsheet out of the cleat: if the jib is backed for too long it will spin the boat through the tack too fast and make it impossible for you to catch up.
- Eyeball the trapeze handle so you know exactly where you are headed on the exit.
- Focus on where you want your body weight to end up. Were you trapezing near the shroud, or further back because of the waves? When you land on the new side, be in that place for fast speed in a straight line.
- The priority is always boatspeed, so think how you can positively impact that through the tack, or how you might be slowing it down. Possible questions: Are you doing a bit of a wheelie through the tack? If so, it would be better if your body weight was further forward. Are you and your helm synchronised when you cross the boat? If not, you should be.

Windy Tack

In terms of process nothing much changes but the helm will steer through the tack slower and you simply need to make sure that you are on top of your stuff otherwise a capsize is generally the only outcome.

Before you drop the jibsheet, double check it's pulled though and clear; make sure that you are definitely unclipped from the trapeze gear.

Your absolute priority is to get the old jibsheet uncleated: it will become less loaded as the boat steers into the wind and so easier to uncleat. If you are struggling to uncleat it, or have got behind, now is the time to shout to your helm and get them to slow down the turn because, if you go through head to wind without it uncleated, the jib will back, catch and you will go swimming.

As you exit the tack, it might be that you have got to the new windward side in plenty of time so, if needed, take a second to pause here and don't run straight out causing the boat to heel to windward.

Ideally it would be in total balance but in truth it might be good to go out with a bit of windward heel so that, as the boat gets down to angle, you are already loaded up on the new side to catch the power.

Asymmetric Trapeze Tack

All that Saskia has said above is relevant to those trapezing on an asymmetric dinghy, but we are aiming for standing up off the wire (as described on p30-31) rather than swinging in. Swinging in to sitting is OK when you are starting out, but not what to have as your goal…

Learning your footwork is key and trying to maintain this in windy weather (waves) is tricky and only possible with practice. A simple mantra like 'aft foot first' to remind yourself how to start a tack will help the sequence run as planned.

It is different for all teams but our tacking technique in trapezing conditions is for the crew to cross the boat as fast as possible on to the new wire and for the helm to believe that the crew will hit the wire as planned to enable them to confidently power up quickly out of the tack even if the helm has not made it out on to the wire fully yet. Tacking can otherwise become a slow and non-competitive manoeuvre as each person waits for the other. The crew has to trust that there will be sufficient power in the sails to balance them when they hit the wire and only if they are out on the wire can the helm get the boat borne off and sailing fast on the new tack. For this reason, it is more important that the helm concentrates on steering and sheeting rather than getting their own weight fully out.

I would recommend a land drill with your boat rigged up and securely supported so you can practise the wire-to-wire manoeuvre over and over with a stable platform and time to think it all through. With repetition, the movement will become instinctive and you will be able to increase the range of conditions in which you can complete a tack fast and accurately. If you get someone to video you while you are doing it you will have a reminder of what to do on the water.

Asymmetric Trapeze Tack

From trapezing on the beat

Move up towards standing

So both of you are standing

Begin to move across the boat

Duck under the boom

Move towards the other side

Step onto the rack

Onto the outer rack

And out on the wire again

Gybing is when the back of the boat travels through the wind and the boom and sail will quickly snap over from being full of wind on one side to full of wind on the other. It is the manoeuvre of choice when going downwind.

However, unlike the tack, with the gybe, there is often the added complication of a third sail: the spinnaker or gennaker, but let's start without that complication.

Gybing Without A Spinnaker

A few double-handed dinghies won't have a spinnaker downwind but may have a jib stick. Going downwind in such boats, typically the helm will be on the windward side and the crew will be on either side depending on the conditions and your angle to the wind. But whichever side you are sitting, you are likely to need to be on the opposite side on completion of the gybe.

The basic gybe, when you are learning to crew, is like the basic tack: essentially you want your weight to transfer in harmony with the turning circle of the boat and your helmsperson, to balance out the pressure in the sails.

- Pre-gybe, pull the slack out of your windward jibsheet and take the jibsheet out of the leeward cleat. If the jib is goose-winged (set on the opposite side from the mainsail), it can stay that way through the gybe but, if you have a jib stick, you can choose to deal with it pre or post gybe.
- As the turn begins, and not goose-winged, let go of the jibsheet and get hold of the previous windward jibsheet.
- Balance your weight transfer across so that the boat stays level without any heel on the entry or exit. This will be a quicker movement in the gybe than the tack because the sails are powered up on one side, flip over quickly and then are immediately powered up on the other side.
- Travel across the boat facing forwards or backwards, one will naturally make sense depending on the boat.
- When the boat has completed its turn, balance the boat on the new gybe and either pull in the new jibsheet (if not goose-winged) or goose-wing the jib on the new windward side, setting the jib stick (if you have one).

The process will vary in speed depending on whether you are gybing run-to-run (slower) or reach-to-reach (faster). It will also depend on the wind strength and wave conditions.

But, as with tacking, you will soon move on from this basic approach and realise that the gybe is a great place to get a nice roll on the hull, so you can pull it flat on the exit and get good acceleration back up to your pre-gybe speed.

The windward roll that you induce on the entry to the gybe will also help the boat's steering for the gybe so it's important to get it right in terms of tempo and amount. Importantly don't over roll it as it can easily lead to a difficult amount of heel to take off on the new side, which actually misses the opportunity for acceleration. It is very boat shape specific but, as a rule, you don't want much more than the edge of the boat (gunwale) just touching the water: anymore and you are likely to take on water.

Basic gybe

From running with the jib goose-winged

Start the turn and balance the boat

The boom will come over

To the other side while you balance the boat

Moving more central as the helm sits down

Get the jib goose-winged again

Hand the jibsheet to the helm

The helm takes the jibsheet

And sail off on the new run

Roll gybe

From the run on one gybe

Stay central as the turn begins

Then increase the heel to windward

So the boat heels further

On maximum heel as the boom comes across

When the boom is across, start to pull the boat upright

So the sails begin to fill

Get the boat level & sails filling

And resume sailing on the new gybe

Gybing With A Symmetric Spinnaker

Basic Process

In contrast to the non-spinnaker boat, in a spinnaker boat going downwind, as the crew, you will be on the windward side with full visibility of the spinnaker. In this position, be as ready as possible for the gybe to limit your preparation time, mostly so that you don't alert competitors behind you. In the 470 this would mean having the lazy jibsheet cleated on the windward side with all the slack taken out, and the tail end of the guy pulled through into the boat with any slack taken out. Ideally the first external sign that you are gybing is as the helm steps across to the windward side, inducing windward heel and initiating the bear away.

The basic process with a double-ended spinnaker pole is as follows:

- Trim the kite perfectly, which will involve easing the sheet and pulling the guy as you 'rotate' the spinnaker round to windward, matching the rate of turn of the steering.
- Whilst doing this, with your guy hand, uncleat / free whatever system you have holding down your guy. It will either be hooked under something on the shroud, hooked under a fairlead at the entrance to a cleat or have an independent twinner block and cleat. This will suddenly create a lot of slack in the system so be ready to take that up on your guy arm.
- At some point during this procedure the helm will take over the old guy, and you continue trimming the old sheet.
- As you are ducking for the boom, pull it over using the kicker with your front hand.
- Get your weight in the right position for what the boat needs for maximum speed, which might be to flatten or to keep the heel on.
- Head straight to the new guy (whilst dropping the old sheet) either pulling on the twinner or placing it under the hook. Be careful not to disturb the set of the spinnaker with this movement, especially if it is light winds.
- Unclip both ends of the pole using the string on the pole, thump the mast end off the ring.
- Keep positive weight down on the pole as you swing the pole through, so it doesn't unhook from the middle.
- Move the old mast end to the new guy and clip it on causing minimum disturbance to the kite.
- Push the pole out towards the windward clew corner of the kite and clip the other end on to the mast.
- Grab the new sheet from your helm and sit down in unison. There might be the opportunity for an aggressive or gentle flatten (depending on the conditions) on the sit down which, if you pump the spinnaker in coordination, will result in an acceleration.
- Get straight back on to trimming the kite

Preparing to gybe at London 2012 © Thom Touw

From your normal position on the run

Release the guy, keep trimming the kite

Roll the boat to windward as you rotate the kite around to windward

Pull the boom over and head straight to pull the twinner on

The mainsail fills on the new side

Go for the spinnaker pole and flatten the boat for an acceleration

Attach the pole to the new guy

Push the pole out, attach to the uphaul and mast

Take control of the spinnaker again

accurately: normally it will need easing out.

The priority through all of this is that the spinnaker stays flying so do it as fast as possible but also as gently as possible. If the spinnaker has collapsed and you can help get it flying again, try by poking the pole out before you clip it onto the mast.

If you have a single-ended pole, you can follow the procedure above, but you will need to bring the pole back into the boat, attach the new guy to the outward end and push the pole out again. Alternatively, you might take the pole in before the gybe and then re-set once the gybe has been completed.

Communication

Similar to the tack, we always have a '2', '1', 'Go' into the gybe. But because you are likely to be defending the boats behind it might be more subtle than that, and no preparation will be done on the countdown, it just signifies the tempo. Through the gybe there will be a series of 'Gots' as you transfer responsibility for the sheet and guy between you and the helm. If you are in a tactical battle, it's helpful if the helm tells you pre gybe that you might be defending high on the exit, you will then know to get your weight up quicker and flatten the boat.

Who 'pops' the top batten will probably change through the wind range. It is easiest to do when the boat is at the correct sailing angle, when there is power in the sails and whilst flattening the boat. Trying without any of those 3 is difficult and probably a waste of time. So, in a basic gybe, the helm doing it on the sit down is the easiest but communicate that it is happening, so the crew knows to pull down in sync with a boom pull in from the helm.

Light Wind Roll Gybe

The basic process will be exactly the same, but you have a lot more time as it takes a surprising amount of time to steer the boat through the gybe angle in the light wind, which might be near 170°, so be patient. Your weight needs to stay on the old

windward side to keep the heel on and help the boat steer.

Ideally the spinnaker will stay flying throughout, which largely depends on whether you have managed to float it round the forestay, without it getting caught on anything, and in time with the steering. Making sure the old spinnaker sheet is untangled and clear to run through the blocks without any friction is a key part of that. As you have ducked for the boom, pull it over using the kicker: the boat will still need to get up to angle so stay on the leeward tank.

If it's very light conditions your weight needs to stay down to leeward whilst you are transferring the pole: it's a bit awkward as the mast is in the way and blocking your view but keeping leeward heel to help the sails fill with wind is paramount. Remember to push the pole out forward towards the forestay, rather than sideways, as the angles you are sailing downwind are large.

The speed, energy and timing of flattening the boat are totally dependent on how much wind you have got. In super-light conditions there will probably be very little in the way of a pull down: just settle into your new angle with minimum disruption to the sails.

If it's really light and any thoughts of flying the spinnaker through the gybe have been abandoned (honestly, sometimes it's just too hard) just get a good amount of roll so that you can pop the batten at the first try when you sit down, this will give a small puff of wind into the kite and get it pulling again.

When it's still light but with a bit more wind, when you have done the pole, focus on a steady squeeze down which builds power as it goes but doesn't result in over flattening and shaking everything you might have gained out of the sails.

As it gets windier you can go for an aggressive flatten as you initially cross the boat, before the pole, to get your first squirt of speed.

As the wind builds, the light wind roll gybe, turns into a roll gybe and then your standard gybe. The routine is exactly the same for them all; just the point at which you flatten the boat is different.

From your normal position on the run

Roll the boat into the turn

Onto the new gybe

Grab the spinnaker pole, keeping the leeward heel

Attach the new guy to the pole

Push the pole out

Clip the pole onto the mast, keeping the heel on through all these moves

Take control of the spinnaker again and, if you have the power, squeeze the boat flat

Windy Gybe

The most important part of a windy gybe, whatever boat you are sailing, is to keep the boatspeed up at all times. Any slow bits load the rig so chances of a nosedive or capsize are higher. It's really important, when you are thinking about a gybe, that none of your preparation slows the boat down, so try to keep the boat tidy and ready when you get time sailing in a straight line. If you are surfing on a wave, tidy up the slack in the guy or slide forward and grab the twinners so they are next to you. Hopefully It will still be tidy when you come to gybe. So, focus on sailing the boat fast until the gybe is called, normally when you are surfing at maximum speed on a wave.

Preparation, although limited, is:
- Guy with as much slack taken out as possible and laid over the traveller bar so the helm can access it easily without standing up and unbalancing the boat.
- Twinner as near to you as possible.
- Shift your bottom as inboard as possible keeping your shoulders out so that your weight is more over your feet.

The helm will call the gybe and get the old guy in their tiller hand, while positively flicking the mainsail over using the mainsheet: they might need your help with this if it's really windy. As soon as there is no pressure in the mainsail your weight needs to be off the side deck.
- Duck and undo the twinner. As it's windy your weight will be a lot further back, so the boom will be lower.
- Get your weight over to the new windward side.
- Snap the new twinner on as fast as possible. Keeping the spinnaker pinned in and close to the boat keeps the whole manoeuvre under control. If the kite billows out and the twinner is not on it risks a capsize.
- Your first priority is making sure the boat is stable and you are not going to nosedive – make sure your weight is far enough back.
- When there is a suitable wave, dive forward and get the pole done as quickly as possible.

It might take a few goes, if your bow is going down a big wave dive backwards to pop the bow.

Those 3 gybes should get you through most situations and conditions in a symmetric spinnaker gybe. It would be impossible to describe all the different combinations of entry angle and exit angle that you will be doing, so take bits and try them out to develop what is best for your team and boat and also the course configurations you are likely to race.

When you are building all your boat handling processes try to keep them as simple as possible in terms of preparation and communication. The number one priority is always to keep the boat going as fast as possible. But also, don't get obsessed by perfect boat handling: it is a really important element and yes, bad boat handling can result in a race-ending disaster, but balance the time and energy you put into training your boat handling with an eye on the overall gains you need to make.

Gybing With An Asymmetric Spinnaker – Hiking Boat

The skill of gybing an asymmetric spinnaker on a hiking boat is underpinned by the same need for preparation and maintenance of speed as their symmetric counterparts. On the other hand, the kinetics and trim required is quite different. Broadly speaking, the crew has a lot more to concentrate on than the helm in an asymmetric class!

As Saskia said, from both a tactical and ease perspective, it is very useful to be able to be ready to gybe without changing what you and the helm look like from outside the boat. If you are difficult to read, your competitors will find it hard to predict and outwit you and, if you can keep sailing fast until the last moment, the manoeuvre will be easier and quicker. I therefore like to have all sheets nicely laid out and ready at all times (not wrapped around my feet or hooked on anything!), so that my journey from one gybe to the other is

Flap the spinnaker if you need to lose some power to finish a windy gybe

mapped out, consistent and stress-free.

One major difference between symmetric and asymmetric spinnakers is that an asymmetric is much like a big jib, attached to the boat at the tack, while a symmetric one floats freely.

An asymmetric spinnaker will always collapse at some point during a gybe. Similar to tacking, this makes the exit to the manoeuvre critical because how the crew gets the sail filling on the new gybe will dictate how much distance and speed is sacrificed to pull it off. Often regardless of the class, crews have two preferred techniques for gybing:

1. Conventional:
- At the start of the manoeuvre (when the boat starts to bear away), the crew starts to ease the existing working sheet and grabs the lazy sheet as close to its block as possible.
- As the boom comes across the boat and you travel to your new position, you release the old working sheet and take the new one with you.
- You will need to scoop up at least a couple more armfuls of sheet as you move, and this will essentially drag the clew of the sail around the forestay and onto the new gybe.
- After the gybe, as the boat is luffed onto its new course, the crew's eyes are fixed on the spinnaker and any signs of life.
- As soon as the luff 'comes alive' and is stirred by the wind, the crew must ease the sheet to allow the new breeze to flow through it (often referred to as the 'pop' due to the satisfying noise and acceleration).

Cleat the jib on the new side

Release old spinnaker sheet

Pull in the new spinnaker sheet

To fill the spinnaker on the new gybe

Pull the boat upright

Start sailing on the new gybe

2. The 'Blow Through':

This technique requires some honing and is not always the best option (particularly in windy conditions), however it does allow for accurate crew movement, frees up a hand for the jibsheet until the last minute and can make an older kite 'pop' onto the new gybe better.

- As the helm bears away into the gybe and after the initial ease of the spinnaker sheet, rather than reaching for the lazy one right away, the crew actually sheets the working one on, thereby pulling the clew inboard slightly.
- When the boom has gone across, the asymmetric kite will then be blown towards the forestay / jib.
- Now a quick jerk on the old sheet will make the sail back.
- When you do this, make sure you have the new sheet to hand because you will then instantly release the old one (before it is loaded up) and whip the clew onto the new side (at the perfect trim, of course!).

From one gybe

Keep the kite filling

Don't release the sheet

So the kite backs

And half blows through with some help from pulling the sheet

To pop on the new side

Throughout these two methodologies, you will have noticed that I have not addressed what to do with the jib. This is because the spinnaker is the bigger, more powerful and therefore your priority throughout the gybe. How a crew gets the jib through the manoeuvre is a question of preference.

Some like to pre-cleat the lazy sheet before the gybe (as on a symmetric boat), some prefer to pre-sheet the jib beforehand so that it does not need attention after the gybe and some like to deal with the spinnaker sheets, body movement and jibsheets at once. Over the years, I have used all these techniques but, as I have become more familiar with the boat, I have settled on the following mixture:

Light winds:

Because my preferred straight-line position is kneeled by the jib cleats, I like to pre-cleat the lazy jib sheet before the gybe, so that I can simply uncleat the working one in the gybe and then trim to course afterwards. This means that the jib blows across but is not over sheeted when you want the boat to accelerate away from the gybe. Any pre-cleating and pre-sheeting will come at the detriment to **speed** which, in all conditions, **is our friend.**

Medium to heavy winds:

In these conditions, the boat is planing and I am generally positioned further away from the jib sheeting points, so I like to take the spinnaker sheet and jibsheet across the boat with me, dealing with both at once. I have continuous jibsheets that allow me to uncleat the old side, cleat the new side and trim it on simply by twisting my wrist and not letting go once, all the while following the conventional spinnaker gybe.

This all might seem a little complex, however, there is no substitute for applied theory so go sailing, have a try, re-read the text and watch your confidence grow. You will soon realise that it is all relatively simple and great fun.

Do bear in mind that, in windier conditions, the crew's weight movement is quite different and exaggerated compared to in a symmetric craft. As the wind increases, you will find yourself transitioning from a relatively static gybing process in light winds to one where you need to get forward of the thwart and around the mainsheet in the middle (all before the boom goes across and you are needed on the new side). Practising your technique based on the helm's and your own preference is essential.

Remember to make sure that the boat is flat prior to the gybe otherwise the boat will slow down when the helm bears away, which is bad because speed is our friend. Some teams prefer to have a countdown as Saskia describes, however I like to cast my eyes down from the luff of the kite to the bowsprit and use its movement to leeward as my cue to dance.

The crew must then unweight themselves from their hiking position and begin their journey across the boat to the new side while gybing the spinnaker and jib. With practice, you will gain a feel for keeping the boat flat throughout the entire manoeuvre – a little leeward heel as you exit the gybe is not the end of the world as long as the helm retains control.

Despite all the practising and repetition, I still find it useful (even still in an RS200) to map out where my feet will go during the manoeuvre, particularly if I am tired.

You might drop a sheet every now and again. If this happens, do not deviate or delay your movement. Your weight is critical to your safe (and dry!) passage and, although the gybe might not end up being as perfect as planned, it is easier to sort out if the boat is upright and not capsized.

You may have noticed that much of my guidance on crewing does not read like an instruction manual. This is intentional. Unlike skiffs and other single trapeze boats, the sheeting positions and cockpit layouts of hiking dinghies vary greatly, as do the styles of gybe throughout the classes and conditions. A universal step-by-step guide, with every detail of the team's actions described, is therefore a difficult process to write accurately. I have written this in the gybing section as this is the manoeuvre that crews frequently find the most emotive – develop your technique around your boat, what you feel confident with and your helm's style and preference.

Gybing With An Asymmetric Spinnaker – Trapeze Boat

Once again, in an asymmetric trapeze boat, the key principles remain the same as other types of boat – keep boatspeed up throughout the gybe.

However, the specific technique in light wind compared to heavy wind is very different. Land drill can again be hugely useful – practising and memorising the footwork and sheeting to cross the boat the same way every time on a nice stable platform.

Light Wind Gybe

Downwind you will need to be in front of the mast for correct trim of the boat. You will be sat as far forward as possible in the lightest breeze, edging back as the wind builds. Ideally sit just far enough out on the side so that you can see the kite to keep it perfectly trimmed – just on the point of the luff curling at all times. It is very important for the helm that they can judge how deep to steer the boat on the angle of the kite luff.

When it is time to gybe (subtly if you are defending on boats behind), get the helm to pass you the bight of the spinnaker sheet on the new side (they should be sat forward too, so will be right next to it) – this is better than you reaching or moving aft to get it and disturbing the trim. Take the slack out of the new sheet. We have a call 'ready to gybe' from helm and 'ready' from me when I am prepared. When the helm picks the exact moment to gybe he counts down 3, 2, 1 to 'gybe' (when the boom comes over):

- 3 – this is the cue to stand facing aft in front of the mast. Take care that the kite doesn't collapse. Move smoothly and gently to minimise slowing the boat down.
- 2 – the boat is bearing away: give a small

sharp tug on the old kite sheet before you start pulling in quickly on the new sheet.

- 1 – keep pulling the new kite sheet round and step over the jibsheet as the jib flips to the new side, the kite should be sheeted hard on the new side momentarily.
- Gybe – the boom goes over and you need to be on the new windward side and immediately easing the kite sheet to set and fill the kite as the boat powers up on the new gybe.
- Sit gently back down on the new side and focus on kite trimming and calling pressure in the kite to the helm.

Windy Gybe

In windy weather we are aiming to do a wire-to-wire gybe.

The boat will be moving fast and covering a lot of distance in a short space of time so planning ahead and anticipating a gybe is all important. Ask the helm to keep you informed of their plan so you are not caught out – you should be focussed on the kite and trimming it perfectly rather than looking around at other boats.

When you know a gybe is approaching, start to gather the slack out of the lazy kite sheet so you have both sheet ends in hand. Keep flat wiring to keep maximum speed and then:

- 'Ready to gybe' – if you are locked in the back footloop, take your foot out the loop and disentangle from your helm, edging forward on the rack to gain a little separation.
- 'Ready' – when you are set with kite sheets gathered tight in aft hand and the loop of slack thrown down behind you, clear of your body – make this call as soon as you are ready and be clear.
- 3 – Reach up with your arm and raise yourself up slightly on the trapeze adjuster if you need to. Maintain a straight body for maximum righting moment for as long as possible. The boat needs to be kept flat at this point (this is the helm's job) to enable the bear away.
- 2 – Reach for the trapeze handle, bend your knees and bring yourself dynamically up to

Asymmetric Trapeze Gybe

From one gybe

Go for the handle

Step into the boat

Move into the cockpit

Go for the new side while trimming the kite

Step onto the new rack

Bend your legs

Come up to standing

Cross under the boom

Kite blows through

Go out with the trapeze

Hook on

standing on the rack tube. As you stand up and move in to the boat, raise your aft hand with the kite sheet in it up above your head to prevent an ease in the sheet that would otherwise result from you moving in.

- 1 – Step in and on to the gunwale with your aft foot and then to the nearside of the cockpit floor with your forward foot. Let go of the trapeze handle as you move and bend and reach down with your forward hand to pick up the new kite sheet next to the block.
- Gybe – duck down facing forward, bring your aft leg to the old leeward side of cockpit floor – wide stance so stable. As soon as you've pulled one arm full on the new kite sheet, drop the original bight with the aft hand and pull a good three or four armfuls quickly as the boom comes through.
- As soon as the boom has cleared your head and you have pulled the kite round to the new side, step up to the new windward gunwale, reaching for the trapeze handle as you go, face towards the trapeze / side of boat. Step out to the rack with the other foot.
- Rotate on your outer foot to turn your body to face into the boat while bringing your other foot out on to the rack too (now your aft foot).

- Drop back so you are hanging off one arm holding the trapeze handle so your body is held straight and tall. Now raise your hips up and with your kite sheet hand bring the trapeze loop to your harness to clip on.
- Ensure the kite is trimmed correctly, this will probably mean easing the kite a little as it is better to go through the gybe with the kite trimmed too tight than too loose and unstable.
- Adjust the height of the trapeze if you need to but then remove both hands from trapeze handle and lie back, shoulders down.
- Move your weight aft and return to the footloop as soon as your helm is locked in to theirs. Wire low for maximum stability.

To begin with, and even when experienced in rough windy conditions, it may not be practical to get straight out on the wire after the gybe. The most important thing is to have the kite properly trimmed as soon as possible on the new gybe, so the boat can accelerate and become stable again. If you can't go straight out on the wire, just aim to get your weight out as far out as possible on the new side – which may be sat on the rack. In this situation you can hook on while sitting down and push yourself out.

A windy asymmetric gybe (From Asymmetric Sailing)

CHAPTER 8
Symmetric Spinnakers

There are a number of ways that symmetric spinnakers in boats are set up, hoisting from a bag within the boat, to a chute out of the front. As my experience is mostly in a 470 (2 kite bags, either side of the mast in the cockpit) my descriptions will focus on that.

Preparation

The much-argued pole situation… the 470 stores a single pole within the boat (not on the boom). I always had the pole ends facing up when flying the spinnaker – I haven't got a reason for this other than I always did and couldn't switch, but there is actually a good argument for having pole ends facing down: if your pole ends jam open, there is a chance that your guy rope will stay in. I had a continuous bit of rope from one pole end to the other, with a small amount of slack in it.

Give your pole ends a good rinse through if you are sailing in salt water and NEVER use your pole to push you off the bottom if you've run aground: sand and mud will ruin the ends. When you are replacing pole ends, make sure you drill into a solid plastic bit of the pole end and not into the spring mechanism. Consider using short grub screws rather than a rivet just for ease of swapping broken pole ends out.

In the 470 we sew stoppers into the spinnaker sheets that effectively provide an automatic guy position. There is discussion about the best place for these: do you have these set for the reach, so that, when twinner is max on, the pole is sitting on the forestay? Or do you have them set shorter, so that when you hoist onto a run, or out of a gybe,

Where I stored the spinnaker pole in the 470

Fireballs store the spinnaker pole on the boom

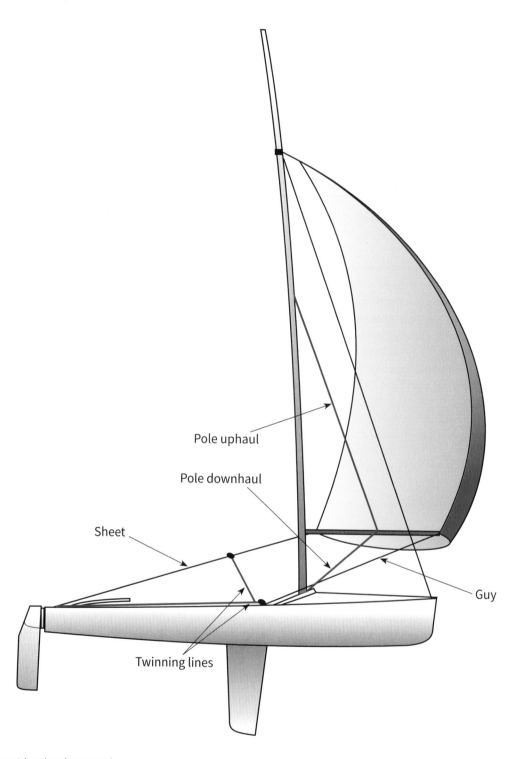

Pole uphaul

Pole downhaul

Sheet

Guy

Twinning lines

Symmetric spinnaker control system

Spinnaker guy with a stopper sewn for correct position for the run

Guy in eased off position for the reach so it sits just off the forestay

and it gives room to thread it through the boat. However, this never seemed to worry other 470 legends who stored it on the starboard side, as it meant more weight on the starboard side off the start line!

Alternatively, you may store your spinnaker pole along the boom, have a twin pole system and a host of different ways of rigging the pole up. If you don't know what to do, talk to the other sailors in your fleet, find out what they do and why. Experiment with the different options.

I don't think any of these things particularly matter performance wise, they are personal preference. Figure out what works best for you but be mindful: it's surprisingly hard to switch once you get used to something.

the pole will sit 60cm (2ft) back from the forestay and the kite will catch with wind? But this means that on a reach you can't pull your twinner to max down. My preference is for the latter but leave the tail in front of the stopper long enough to allow for the rope to shrink. You can always leave a bit of a tail when you tie it off at the spinnaker clew but, if you go too short, it will be impossible to set the twinner in the right place for the reach. Also put some calibration on your twinner, so you know how much to leave off for the reach.

A final thing, which is personal preference, is where do you keep your spinnaker pole? I was not an ambi-poler (able to work with the pole stored in either side of the boat) so always had it stored down the port side. My reason for this was that the set play hoist was with me on the starboard side

The Hoist

Contrary to what you might think, the most important part of hoisting the spinnaker is not getting the kite to the top as fast as possible but keeping boatspeed on through the turn and hoist: so timing and communication on the bear away are the most important things.

Good hoists start before the race, so make sure you've rigged your spinnaker up correctly and 'run' the tapes: that is pulling the starboard tape hand to hand, from the head until you reach the clew. And do the same again with the port tape. However, clean you think your drop was at the end of the previous race, please always do this! There is nothing worse than the shame of a twist on the first hoist when it's only your fault!

Reaching Hoist, Leeward Bag

In preparation, pull out some of the guy; helm puts on the twinner

Come off the trapeze on the bear away

Unhook from the trapeze

Attach the guy to the pole, call '1'

Attach the uphaul to the pole, call '2'; the helm will start to hoist

Push the pole out as the helm hoists

Attach the pole to the mast

Grab the sheet

Get the spinnaker filling

Reaching Hoist, Leeward Bag

This is the basic hoist, which you will set up for pre-start assuming you are doing a port rounding at the top. Ideally you will have had a starboard tack approach to the windward mark.

- On your final port approach, check the halyard is clear of the end of the spreaders.
- On your final starboard approach pull the clew of the kite out of the bag, get your helm to pull the twinner on to the mark (pre-start – always do a practice hoist onto a reach so you know where this is and it gives you the chance to leave a tail on the spinnaker sheet if it is too long).
- As you bear away, trim the jib. If you are over max power, let the helm get settled in terms of centreboard and kicker and come in on their call. They will match any further bear away to you coming in. If you can raise your trapeze hook in this process it will make getting out post hoist easier, but don't waste any time on it. If you are under max power, go straight for the pole.
- As soon as you are off the wire, you are down power and anyone who does this quicker than you is back up to speed faster: SO MAKE IT HAPPEN!
- Feed the pole out under the jibsheet, straight onto the guy (call '1'), middle pole hook on (call '2', which is when the helm can go for the halyard to hoist) and onto the mast. If it's windy getting it on to the mast might be difficult. Get a stable base with your legs so the spinnaker's flapping doesn't boss you around, deep breath and get it done.
- From here it will be a race to the spinnaker sheet between you and your helm. If the wind is light enough you can have the sheet cleated in the port cleat tidy in the boat, so the spinnaker will automatically be sheeted, but make sure this in uncleated during your preparation if it is windier.
- As soon as you have the spinnaker sheet do whatever is needed for optimum boat heel.

This might be staying down to leeward and generating some heel for an accelerating pull down to windward or, if it's windier, grab the trapeze handle and power out on to the windward side, letting the sheet slip through your hand as you go, as you are likely to be over-sheeted. If you managed to get your trapeze hook height up a bit on the bear away then you can go straight onto the hook, otherwise get your helm to hook you on or take the spinnaker sheet whilst you hook on.

Reaching Hoist, Windward Bag

This can be hugely costly in terms of tactical positioning during a race, so it is worth spending some time getting your process right because sometimes it will be unavoidable.

There are 2 ways:

1. 'Chuck it'

There is no preparation to do, you can't have the twinner pre-cleated as it will restrict the throw and risk the spinnaker not getting around the forestay.

- Bear away as before, come in on your helm's call keeping as much height as you can.
- Clear the halyard from the spreader.
- Gather up the kite out of the bag cleanly in a ball and be careful not to put any twists in it. You need to be max forward, next to the mast so the windward shroud doesn't get in your way when you go for the chuck.
- On your call, launch the kite ('2', '1', 'Go') with the focus on looping it round the forestay, not giving it height. On the shout of 'Go' the helm will hoist.
- Go straight to the twinner and then the pole as before. The helm will definitely beat you to the sheet.

The 'chuck it' definitely has a maximum wind strength above which it won't work and the spinnaker will just get blown back in your face. In that scenario you need to go for the big bear away (see p66).

Reaching Hoist, Windward Bag

Come in off the trapeze on the bear away

Unhook from the trapeze

Stand up

Lean right forward to chuck

Attach the guy to the pole

Attach the uphaul

Grab the spinnaker

Get all the spinnaker in your hands

Count '2, 1, Go' – chuck on 'Go' as the helm hoists; go straight for the twinner

Go for the pole

Push the pole out and attach to the mast

Start trimming the spinnaker

2. Big Bear Away

On '2' count, when you have the pole on the middle clip, the helm will go for a big bear away, pretty much to downwind and hoist so the kite naturally blows round the front of the forestay as you luff back up. There is a windspeed when this is your only option but beware as it causes a big positional loss.

Come in off the trapeze on the bear away

Set the twinner (if it's not done) and go for the pole

Attach the guy to the pole, call '1'

Attach the uphaul to the pole, call '2'

Push the pole out as the helm begins to hoist

Attach the pole to the mast

Grab the spinnaker sheet

Get the spinnaker flying

Hook on ready to head up again onto the reach

Running Hoist, Leeward Bag

The process for this hoist is the same as hoisting onto a reach.

The most important bit for this manoeuvre is the boat balance: sailing upwind you need to be on the wire or max hiked as you are coming in on the layline but get your balance right so that you avoid being slungshot round the front or end up in the water like a sea anchor.

The potential error on this hoist is the spinnaker getting caught on the jib as it goes up. Ease the jib on the bear away but, just as you come in for the pole, oversheet it 15cm (6in) so that the kite can shoot up outside of it.

Pull out some of the guy

The helm pulls the twinner on

Come in off the trapeze on the bear away

Attach the guy to the pole, call '1'

Push the pole out

Attach the uphaul to the pole, call '2'; helm will start to hoist

Push the pole out and attach to the mast

Get the spinnaker flying

Settle into your normal position

Running Hoist, Windward Bag

The biggest risk on this hoist is the spinnaker being hoisted into the pole hook and ripping or a spinnaker head hoisted into your face or hand, because it really hurts! Ideally you will have time for the twinner preparation on the layline but, if not, the basics are the same: boat heel on the turn is the priority to help the steer round the windward mark.

- Unhook from your harness and have your body weight on your arm: then you have much more control of where your body weight ends up as you swing into the boat. There might be enough wind so that you can just slide onto the side. If not, keep your bottom high, don't touch the deck and transfer your weight straight onto your feet by the centreline.

- Twinner onto position, pole end on guy, the kite will probably be being hoisted in front of your face at this point: keep it out of the way, whilst grabbing the hook and pulling that backwards towards you.

- If it's lightish winds it could be worth pushing the pole out and forward, so it catches some wind getting the leeward clew past the forestay, before you hook the pole onto the mast.

Come in off the trapeze on the bear away

Set the twinner (if it's not done) and go for the pole

Attach the guy to the pole

Attach the uphaul to the pole as the helm hoists the spinnaker, pulling the uphaul back towards you

Push the pole out

Attach the pole to the mast

Start to control the spinnaker

Rotate the spinnaker round to windward for the run

Running Hoist, Gybe Set

The most important thing with a gybe set is to keep as much boatspeed on throughout and not kill it with steering or bad boat heel: rushing to get the pole on is likely to cause that.

- As always, windward heel around the turn and gybe; on the exit of the gybe, flatten the boat properly to get your pump as you would any gybe.
- Transfer the jibsheet over through the gybe.
- If you have a spare hand through the gybe, grab an armful of spinnaker clew out of the bag in front of you which will help reduce the friction of getting the new twinner on. But make sure it's not so much that the sheet drops round the front of the boat.
- It's now full speed process of getting the twinner and pole on as with any other hoist.

Routine-wise, the gybe set is no different to the other hoists except that you will feel behind the

Running Hoist, Gybe Set

Come in off the trapeze on the bear away

As you turn into the gybe, pull out some spinnaker

Go for the gybe and pull on the twinner

Adjust the jib and go for the pole

Attach the guy to the pole, call '1'

Attach the uphaul to the pole, call '2'

Put the pole on the mast

Take control of the spinnaker and flatten the boat for an acceleration

Trim the spinnaker

curve and possibly your preparation will have been done for another style of hoist. Keep calm and methodical and go through your process accurately.

Advanced Hoisting

If you approach on or near the port layline it is possible to do some preparation to help the hoist. Pull an armful of starboard clew out of the bag and, if there is time and space, get your helm to reach across and pull on some starboard twinner. With any preparation it is important that you don't do it if it's going to have a massive speed implication on the upwind. Metres and positioning are really important at the entry to a mark and pulling on the twinner can really disrupt the shape of the base of the jib and impact speed which could have a bigger negative effect than being slightly behind on the preparation for the hoist.

Hoisting Troubleshooting

Always check that the halyard is clear of the spreaders pre-hoist, however it will still happen. It is easy to solve if it's the windward side and you are there, just flick it around. If it's on the leeward side, it will probably be pinned by the mainsail, so the main needs to be pulled in enough so it is not pressing on the spreaders, the spinnaker halyard uncleated, pulled down and flicked around the spreaders. It is impossible to do if the mainsail hasn't been pulled in enough.

The Drop

If you are racing an Olympic course (also most championship / open meeting courses), rounding windward marks to port, the default hoist will be a bear away set so, with this in mind, the default drop is a port approach, so you can just drop it into the windward bag. This is the ideal but obviously you will be where you will be at the leeward mark.

Timing is everything in a drop: you don't want to be without the extra sail area for any length of time, but conversely, in most circumstances, it is more costly to cruise past the leeward mark(s)

with your kite still up (which often comes with the added bonus of shouting at each other). This could change in lighter winds, especially if you are going downwind into the tide and would do anything to keep or gain an overlap, and are happy to deal with the drop after the rounding.

In the standard set-up of downwind roles, the crew's responsibility is speed, so a high focus on trimming the kite. In preparation for the leeward mark rounding, it's a bonus if the helm can paint a good picture of the tactical scenario coming into the mark (e.g. 'a boat right on our tail, we need to leave this drop late so they don't get the overlap'; or it could be, 'no threats behind'). The helm will probably call the timing of the drop based on the tactical situation going on around you, BUT it is always the crew's responsibility to pull the plug and go for the drop if you think they are leaving it too late for you to get it all done.

Throughout the process the fundamental of making sure your body weight is in the right place, so the boat can sail as fast as possible, always applies. You might need to get your weight far to leeward to help with turning the corner, or weight back to stop a nosedive on a wave. Whatever interruptions you have, it's important to get back to action as soon as you can. Whilst dropping, be mindful of not twisting your hands over each other and getting the kite into a knot. If you have an old or wet kite it just wants to stick to you and follow your hand around, so give yourself a bit more time on the drop. You'll know if you've done a messy drop, but the priority is to get the boat sailing upwind as fast as possible: there might be the opportunity on the next leg to sort it out. Always run the tapes after the finish, whatever.

If you lose a sheet around the bow of the boat, make a dive for it and try to rescue it. You'll be surprised how effective that can be even if you think it's too late, but its way quicker than the alternative of undoing the sheets. I always tie my spinnaker sheets to the clew with neat bowlines rather than a knot and a hitch, just in case they do end up needing to be untied mid race: a bowline is much easier to undo.

Drop Into Windward Bag

- Pull the lazy part of your jibsheet taut through the cleat and drape it over the centreboard so the area where the pole will be stowed is clear and there is no jibsheet dangerously hanging around the spinnaker bag area.
- The helm takes the sheet and continues flying the kite as you slide forward. Depending on the wind strength you'll either be sitting or, if its lighter, you will need weight more to leeward in anticipation of the helm standing up from the leeward side.
- Use the rope on the pole to unclip the mast and outboard end, as you thump the mast end up / down (depending on which way your clip is mounted) and off the mast.
- Unclip the middle and stow the pole in the boat (for me this would always be on the port side),

making sure it is underneath all other sheets (jib and spinnaker), and control lines that might be across the boat (kicker, cunningham etc.).

- Ideally the helm will still have the kite flying at this point and, if the drop was called too early, you can take a pause and still sail.
- When you are ready to drop, your forward hand goes onto to the guy, inside the shroud, as the helm uncleats the halyard. Take 2 or 3 big armful pulls along the foot, stuffing it into the bag as you go and then armfuls up along the tape towards the head, and then tidy the final bit of the foot into the bag on top, making sure the jibsheet is clear and has not been packed underneath the spinnaker.
- Hook the halyard under any tidy / retainer system you may have and uncleat the twinner.

The helm starts to fly the spinnaker

Go for the pole and detach it from the mast

Take in the pole as the helm flies the spinnaker

Store the pole away

In the bottom of the boat

Grab the guy in your forward hand

Pull the spinnaker in a take hold of the clew

Pull along the foot while the helm releases the halyard

Pull in the spinnaker, 2 armfuls along the foot

Start lowering it into the bag

Pack it away

Until it is all in the bag

Get ready for the rounding

Head up

Past the leeward mark

Drop Into Leeward Bag

This is a tricky drop as you get boxed in by the mainsail, boom and active jibsheet, so there is some room for error. Figure out if it is possible in your boat and weigh up the extra time it takes against what you save on the next hoist. It wasn't something I used on an Olympic course because, by the time we were hoisting on a reach on the second lap, the fleet had generally spread out enough that the cost wasn't worth it. But, if you can / have to:

- Get the pole off early and move your weight down to leeward, under the boom.
- Let the windward twinner off and start gathering the kite up along the bottom. The helm will uncleat the halyard as you start pulling down from above your head, stuffing it in the bag as you go, making sure that you are always stuffing outside the jibsheet.
- Weight back up to windward if it's needed for the bear away gybe.

Other Drops Into Bags

There are a number of other combinations of drop, gybe, rounding:

- Pole off, gybe, drop, rounding
- Gybe, pole off, drop, rounding

The process for doing them is a variation of everything we have discussed and the important thing to get right with them is the communication from the helm and the timing. Invariably your drops will end up being a combination with a gybe or head up happening when you are half way through, so be flexible on what you are doing and where your body weight is to help the boatspeed as much as possible. The golden rule for it all is not to pack the kite over the jibsheet.

Dropping Troubleshooting

If a sheet goes over the bow, firstly dive forwards and do everything to unloop it. As the boatspeed is down this can be surprisingly successful, surprisingly late.

If that fails and the sheet has already gone past the centreboard, get the kite packed so it doesn't blow out and get sailing. As soon as possible, untie the bowline from the offending sheet and pull it through: careful not to lose any bobbles on the way through and don't be too aggressive pulling otherwise you could rip your slot gasket. Once that is done and the sheet is in the boat, get racing properly again, and get your strategy right. At some point up the beat you need to re-thread the sheet, get it around the forestay and re-tied, but pick your moment when you have space and hopefully it won't be too big a loss.

Spinnaker Chutes

All that I have written above is based on using spinnaker bags, although much of what I have said should be useful if you sail a symmetric spinnaker boat which has a spinnaker chute. The chute, in many ways, just makes it easier!

As with spinnaker poles, chutes come in a variety of different types. Some are in front of the forestay and some are behind, usually offset on port to make the usual port rounding and hoist on starboard tack easier.

How you hoist and lower the spinnaker in terms of putting the pole out and pulling the halyard will depend on how they are set up in your particular class or boat. It is impossible to cover every possibility, so I will just give some pointers here.

Preparation

Most of the preparation that I have already covered remains relevant, but with a chute you have one additional line (the downhaul) and the problem of the spinnaker sheets going over the bow is sometimes greater.

The downhaul is attached to the spinnaker and is used to pull the spinnaker down into the chute when dropping the kite. Make sure it is rigged and running properly and doesn't go the wrong side of one of the spinnaker sheets.

With some spinnakers and some chutes there is greater likelihood that the spinnaker sheets will go under the bow when dropping. Some classes rig up devices to decrease the likelihood of that happening. Have a look at the other boats in your class and do what others do.

While still on the bow, it is worth remembering that, with a chute, your expensive spinnaker (often wet and so with increased friction) is pulled past the forestay and associated fittings. Make sure these are taped up to get rid of any potentially ripping sharp edges.

Hoist

The reaching hoist on starboard and the running hoist are really straightforward – the spinnaker is basically where you want it when it is hoisted. Who pulls the spinnaker up and whether the pole is set before, during or after the hoist will depend on your particular class and boat set-up. With some port-offset chutes, the jib can potentially get in the way of the hoist and you may need to cleat this in tight before the hoist or just pull it in when the spinnaker starts to come out of the chute.

The reaching hoist on port tack may be slightly more difficult if you have a port-offset chute behind the forestay. You just need to make sure that the spinnaker gets around the forestay before it fills. Putting out the pole might do this, or it may require some pulling on the spinnaker sheet to pull it round. Obviously the more your helm can bear away, the easier this will be.

Drop

Providing the downhaul is set up correctly, the drop is very easy. Again, who is responsible for and the order of releasing the halyard, pulling the spinnaker down and getting in the pole will be class and set-up dependent and co-ordination will be required between helm and crew. With a port-offset chute, a drop on port tack will be the reverse of the hoist, you will need to get the spinnaker around the forestay and into the chute. Again, bearing away for the drop will make this easier.

If sailing with a symmetric spinnaker with a spinnaker chute, I also recommend that you read the next chapter because most asymmetric spinnakers are operated using a chute and you will be able to pick up some useful tips from Rob and Emma, even if you are not sailing an asymmetric boat yourself.

Dropping a spinnaker into a chute – here in the Mirror (From The Mirror Book)

The act of hoisting and dropping an asymmetric spinnaker is usually a far simpler operation than with a symmetric spinnaker. The asymmetric spinnaker is usually stowed in a chute and very rarely does the crew have to manhandle the sail or the 'pole' (bowsprit) themselves. But typically it is solely the crew's job to hoist and drop the kite.

Asymmetric Hiking Boat

Preparation

On an RS200, the mechanics of the hoist could not be simpler: the crew pulls the halyard and the head of the sail shoots up the mast, while the system is linked to the line that deploys the bowsprit, so it all happens automatically.

Having said that, every one of Saskia's points regarding communication and preparation ring true, so check both with a practice hoist and drop before the day's racing.

Some boats, such as the RS400, do not have a fully automated hoist system and so the pole will need to be extended before starting to hoist the spinnaker. Resisting the temptation to do this too soon, and therefore washing the spinnaker out the chute and into the water, is the greatest challenge, rather than actually incorporating it into your hoist routine.

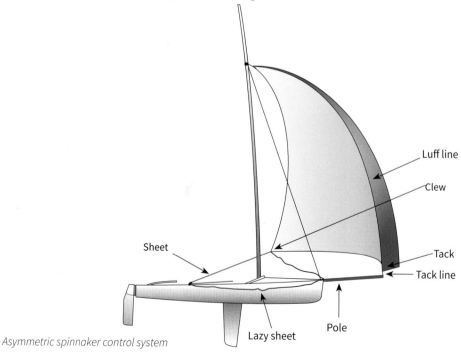

Luff line
Clew
Sheet
Tack
Tack line
Lazy sheet
Pole

Asymmetric spinnaker control system

The Hoist

Hoisting an asymmetric spinnaker can be achieved through one of two ways:

1. Bear Away Hoist

This is when a team chooses to remain on the same tack as you were on when you rounded the mark (usually starboard):

- Firstly, the crew will ease the jibsheet and then the helm will bear away onto a run.
- The crew starts to hoist by pulling the halyard as fast as possible until the head of the sail reaches the sheave in the mast. (TIP: It can be useful to have whipped a mark on the halyard so that you can see when the sail is fully up without having to look up).
- When this has happened, the helm will luff until the kite 'comes alive' and you follow the same procedure with the sheet as after a gybe and assume your straight-line position.

As you get slicker at this manoeuvre as a team, you can look at handing the spinnaker sheet back to the helm in breezier conditions before the mark rounding, so that the kite can be 'popped' sooner. This is also useful in the event you are approaching a hoist where the chute is on the windward side and the clew needs pulling around the forestay.

From the beat

On the bear away, get up and ease the jib

With a powerful stance, start to hoist the kite

Using big armfuls, pull it up and the pole out

Don't look up until you hit your marks

Quickly grab the sheet and trim

2. Gybe Set

This is used when a team chooses to gybe straight after the windward mark, while simultaneously hoisting the spinnaker.

- If the crew can pre-cleat the lazy jibsheet before the mark rounding, they can simply uncleat the leeward one as the helm bears away and forget about it until the boat is sailing on the new gybe.
- Once this is done, the crew can start hoisting the sail as the boat goes through the gybe and then pop the sheet as normal.

Practice will allow you to hone your body movement, timing and how / when the helm luffs after the gybe.

In many classes, easing the mainsail controls (such as the outhaul), is fast downwind. Aside from the kicking strap, I tend to hold off doing this until the spinnaker is up and the boat is sailing downwind. In light and medium conditions, this can sometimes be done on the spreader leg but it is best to check with the helm first.

Reaching Hoist

Asymmetric classes generally sail windward-leeward courses and so reaching hoists are rarely a concern. However, if you do sail a course with reaching (perhaps in handicap racing) or choose to hoist on the spreader leg, then make sure you have a conversation with your helm before the leg begins to assess feasibility. The helm may have to sail a slightly lower angle than they would prefer to enable the crew to hoist and control the kite before heading up to the required course.

The Drop

I have found that the final third of a run is the most testing time for a team's communication because the crew has a lot to do physically while the helm has the best view of the overall situation. As a crew, we want to establish the plan for the approach to the leeward mark as soon as possible, while the helm's inclination is to delay this decision for as long as possible due to the changeability

From the beat

Carry on hoisting on the bear away, uncleating the working jibsheet

When gybed, pull the spinnaker sheet

Get up on the bear away and cleat the lazy jibsheet

Start hoisting the kite

Keep your head and back low so the helm can gybe when they want to

Keep your head down and hoist until you hit your marks

To release the spinnaker from the forestay

And sail away

of a leeward mark scenario (largely due to the unpredictability of other boats).

I like to have a fundamental plan from the helm so I can map things out, however, if things change, it is critical that my crew work is up to the job. There are three fundamental types of drop in an asymmetric scenario, however it is important that, as with gybing, the sheets are untangled beforehand. The helm will generally count down for this manoeuvre, although through practice and repetition, a simple 'OK go' became enough prep from Maria before excecuting.

1. Standard Drop

This is when the boat approaches the leeward mark on the same gybe as it will round on. Then the following process commences:

- Much like a gybe, the helm will bear away so the boat depowers enough for the crew to go down. If it is light winds and you are soaking low, an angle change may not be required.

- While holding the sheet (to keep the sail flying) and downhaul as close to its block as possible with one hand, uncleat the spinnaker halyard with the other. Alternatively, hand the sheet to the helm before the drop (this will mean that they can keep it from falling into the water).

- Release the sheet and begin pulling the sail down into the chute with the downhaul, hand-over-hand as fast as you can.

- TIP: If the halyard keeps re-cleating, a Harken cam can have its springs doubled up or a Spinlock PXR has a tab so that the sailor can tailor how stiff its engagement is. Until you have time to do this, make sure the helm bears away enough to completely depower the spinnaker and keep a close eye on the cleat.

- ADDITIONAL TIP: If you keep getting knots in

Locate the downhaul and get ready for the drop

Pull the downhaul with big powerful armfuls

Pull the spinnaker into the chute

Get your body weight in the right place to help steer the boat

the halyard when dropping, wait until you are onshore and run the line through your hand, while walking away. This will help to get any twists out.

- The game is not over once the sail is tucked away in its chute. If time allows, pull the now loose sheets out the water before the leeward mark. As the helm rounds the leeward mark, move your weight accordingly, pull the controls on and sheet the jib.

- Ideally, you will exit the drop with the boat and crew set up for upwind sailing, however sometimes things get frantic or a halyard re-cleat can slow things down. Regardless, make sure the jib is in and the boat is moving as nicely as it can be upwind; if the helm wants to tack, get that done. When the going is good, start tidying up.

2. Gybe Drop

This is when the spinnaker is dropped and the boat gybes simultaneously, usually while rounding a mark. In this manoeuvre, your body movement fundamentally mirrors that in a gybe except that, rather than sheeting the spinnaker on the new side, the crew uncleats the halyard and drops the spinnaker.

This is a skill that requires a lot of practice to make smooth and advantageous. My main tip with this would be to push as close to the mark rounding as possible with the gybe drop in training and really put yourselves under pressure as a team. This will enable you to establish what is possible because very often, dropping the spinnaker before gybing round the mark is more sensible, particularly in windy conditions. Be warned, you might get wet establishing the parameters!

Locate the downhaul and get ready for the drop

Drop the spinnaker as you roll into the gybe

Pulling the last bit down on the new gybe, trimming the jib and adjusting your body weight

Pull the boat flat as you go onto the beat

3. Gybe-Pop Drop

Occasionally a gybe will be required close to the leeward mark, however dropping before or during the gybe would leave you sailing downwind without a spinnaker for a painfully long time before luffing around. Adding to your armoury the ability to gybe-pop the spinnaker and swiftly drop before the mark will not only open up a wider array of tactical options for the helm, but also enable you to get away with the occasional misjudged layline.

From sailing downwind

Go for the gybe

With the main & spinnaker crossing

To the other side

Get the spinnaker filling

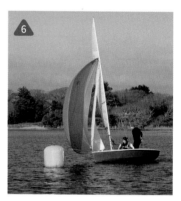

For the last bit to the mark

Then lower the kite

As you round up

And pass the buoy

Asymmetric Trapeze Boat

Preparation

Take care rigging the kite. This is the most common part of boat rigging to get wrong in the haste to launch. Allow enough time to rig calmly and double check what you have done.

There will be a lot of kite to handle and it's a physical job to hoist and drop, so make things as easy as possible with good set-up:

- Having the right length of kite halyard and a good elastic take up will make hoisting and dropping easier and reduce the risk of tangle and knots as you pull on the line.
- Ensure all the blocks in the system spin freely and keep them well rinsed with fresh water after sailing in salt water.
- Tape up or use bicycle inner tube to cover any sharp edges or split rings or shackles that might snag the kite.
- Use a lubricant to help the pole slide in and out with less friction.

Typically, the downhaul end of the spinnaker halyard will attach to a couple of points on the sail. Setting the tail end bowline to a longish length will keep the two eyelets apart as they are pulled into the chute and so spread the size of the bunched area of the kite so it can fit more easily into the chute.

Some physical fitness will be very helpful, best generated by lots of time on the water pulling the kite up & down!

The Hoist

Before the bear away make sure you know whether you will be gybing or not around the windward mark or spreader mark. The helm will usually make that call depending on the boats around you and where the wind is likely to be best on the run.

In any decent breeze, it will not be possible to get the boat to bear away unless you have released the kicker and cunningham in advance. Do this as you approach the windward mark or on the spreader reach if there is one. Calibrate the kicker so that you can let it off the appropriate amount ready for the run. Allow time if you have had the controls on to max as the loads will be high; raise yourself up on the trapeze wire to get a better angle on the lines to the cleats if need be. Try to do this efficiently as you will be losing boatspeed all the time, but you must release the controls before the mark.

Once the call is made to hoist, your sole aim is to get the kite up & set as fast as possible; ideally faster than the crews around you. This requires focus and aggression if you want to win!

1. Bear Away Hoist

The most common hoist is to bear away and set. In windy conditions you will need to keep weight out on the wire to initiate a turn. Ease the jib well out to enable the turn and then pull back in to a downwind setting. When the boat has borne off sufficiently you are free to move into the boat and hoist. The helm may need to make a clear call to you at the right moment to go in.

Agree with your helm who is making the call to hoist after the bear away. In easy conditions you can agree before the mark that the plan is to hoist as fast as possible, so you know your job is to act fast as soon as the bear away is complete. However, if there are waves or chop or you are rounding close with other boats, the helm should make a clear call to 'hoist' when they can judge the waves, so you need to be hand-on halyard ready to go as soon as that call is made.

- Stand over the halyard uphaul block, facing forward, with a wide stable stance. There is a lot of halyard to pull though and you need to take arm over arm pulls on it as fast as you can to get the kite up through the danger zone away from the water to avoid it trawling and the boat coming to an abrupt standstill. Just keep your head down and keep pulling relentlessly without pause until it reaches the top. You will learn how many armfuls this typically is.
- As soon as it's up, reach down to the leeward

Bear Away Hoist

Move into the centre of the boat

With a wide stance, facing forward go for the halyard

Keep your head down and keep pulling until the kite hits the top

Quickly get to the sheet to get the kite pulling and avoiding any twists

kite block and sheet in fast. Best to over-sheet and then ease quickly to set nicely than to have the kite flapping longer and potentially risk a twist.

- Once set, then get quickly out on the trapeze if there is sufficient breeze. Your helm can make a call that it's 'weight forward' or 'single wiring' or 'twin wiring' while you are setting the kite as they have had a few seconds to take in the conditions. Then you know where to move to before your head is up from the hoist.

- Immediately focus on trimming the kite for maximum speed. This is more important than weight being fully out on the wire as the helm can compensate initially by sailing a little lower than optimum, but the boat is up and going rather than stalled.

This hoist can be made more or less easy by the actions of your helm:

- Generally, the hoist is easiest the deeper they run but they will not want to lose too much speed by doing this for long. A very deep run also risks the kite twisting as it goes up.

- If they need to luff up due to the proximity of a leeward boat, then the hoist can get much harder and you may need to shift your weight to the windward side to assist with balance while still pulling the halyard up as fast as possible but from a less ergonomic position. It is sometimes hard to remain civil with your helm in this situation!

- In waves, the helm can help by steering around the waves and heeling the boat slightly to windward to prevent the bundle of kite that

Use big powerful armfuls to get the spinnaker up

Keep going as you hoist through the 'danger zone'

Trim the kite perfectly

And out onto the trapeze

emerges from the chute all at once ending up being grabbed by a wave and probably resulting in a trawl. In some wave conditions it can be virtually impossible to prevent a trawl on one gybe or the other and this may dictate whether you gybe before you hoist at the windward mark.

2. Gybe Set

If the pressure is on the left of the run or you are buried in the pack and need to break off from the starboard 'motorway' then a gybe set might be the best option. A downside, if there are lots of boats behind, is that you will sail in the lee of the boats still on the beat to begin with. Your helm will need to be alert to boats still further back on the beat in case of gybing on to a collision course; you have

few rights here!

The bear away follows the same initiation but ideally you move as fast as possible into the middle of the boat and immediately start hoisting, head well down, as the helm continues a smooth bear away and gybe of the boat. Your aim is to have hoisted quickly enough so that by the time the boom hits the new side you are reaching for the sheet and sheeting in and moving out to the new side on your trapeze in one continuous motion.

One advantage is that, while the boat is pointing dead downwind, the kite should go up nice and fast. However, you are quite dependent on your helm not messing up as you are not in a great position with a half-hoisted kite to help them with the balance of the boat if they don't get it quite right!

Gybe Set

Into the boat on the bear away

Go for the halyard

Hoist as you go into the gybe

Until fully up

Start trimming the sheet

Step out onto the racks

Hold the trapeze handle

Hook on

Out onto the trapeze

The Drop

Again, this manoeuvre wants to be completed as fast as possible to minimise downtime from sailing at maximum speed. As for other dinghies, the timing of the drop will be dictated by the boats around and tactics of the mark rounding. Typically, the helm makes the call but go for the drop if you think they've left it too late as otherwise you'll find yourself hauling it in while they try to sail up the next beat – a whole lot harder and slower than starting the drop 1 second earlier!

Before the drop I usually pass the kite sheet to the helm so that they can continue to get speed on as I move into the boat and it avoids the kite flapping and stowing in the chute with greater potential for a twist on the next hoist. If the helm is unavailable to hand the sheet to then I continue to sheet it as I move in and, as I go for the drop, I put my foot on the sheet to trap it until the kite is mostly in the chute.

After the kite is fully in the chute, pull on both sheets and gather the slack in to the middle of the boat to reduce chance of trailing a sheet upwind.

Immediately be ready to pull the jib in and balance the boat as you round the leeward mark. As your head is down at this point, it is helpful if the helm gives you a countdown to luffing round the mark. The kicker and cunningham can wait until you are settled on the beat and out on the wire.

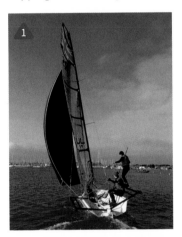
Come in on the bear away

Going to the centre of the boat

Adopt the wide stance

Pull the spinnaker down

And pull...

Until all is packed away

CHAPTER 10
Straight-Line Speed

Boat Set-Up

Boat set-up is a huge topic and I'd recommend referring to *Tuning to Win* for more detail, but a few things to get you started:

- There will be loads of information on the internet about how to set up your boat, and most sailmakers will have a set-up guide for their brand which is the starting point. If you can't find anything, ask the more experienced sailors in the fleet. It's really important to get the basic onshore settings right and create a system so that you can change between them whilst you are on the water.
- With a permanent marker, mark where you are pulling the jib halyard to, record what shroud pin number you are on, make a calibration system for your jibsheet – this is the only way to create a repeatable tuning guide.
- Measure things before you sail and when you come in and keep a record of the conditions and how you were going, building up your own tuning guide.

Upwind Speed

Jib Set-Up

Even though the jib is the small relation to the mainsail, it makes large contribution to your performance upwind and, as the crew, it is your domain. The jib's main job is to accelerate wind on to the leeward side of your mainsail and you need to set the jib slot to get the optimum power from the wind.

In under-powered conditions you are trying to squeeze as much energy from the wind without

The jib slot between the jib and mainsail

making the gap so hard to get through that the wind just doesn't bother. When you are over-powered, you are trying to lose and spill wind from the leech of the jib because the wind strength is too much for the boat to cope with. And in between those two states is 'max power' when your jib leech is set at it's tightest.

Jib control system in the 470 with a jib car (fore & aft)

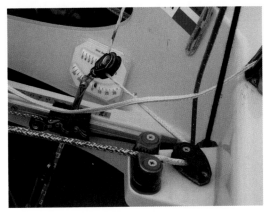

Jib control system in a Fireball with a jib car (sideways) and piston (equivalent of a fore & aft jib car)

Control of the jib leech is a combination of two main elements: the jibsheet and jib car position. You might not have an adjustable jib car in your boat, if so, you would use the windward / lazy jibsheet instead. To understand the effect of the sheet and car, rig up the jib in 6-7 knots of wind and look how the two elements affect the sail. If you pull only jibsheet the leech will be straight, using jib car (or the windward jibsheet) puts a curve in the jib leech. Look at the shape the foot of the jib is making on the foredeck, using jibsheet makes a straight line (a flat jib) and jib car makes a semi-circle (a deep jib). Look how much movement of jibsheet or jib car it takes to change the shape. The object is to mirror the shape of the mainsail as you look at the boat from behind, but as a crew you don't have that viewing perspective when racing.

Three visual tools to get you in the ballpark of correct jib set up are:

1. Make a small mark half way down the luff of your jib (either measure it or fold it in half). Draw an imaginary line from that point to the clew of your jib and with a permanent pen mark the final 10cm (4in) by the clew. The starting point for a powerful sheeting angle is when the jibsheet is a continuation of that pen line. If you are trying to encourage flow over the sail because it's light or get rid of flow because it's windy, then move the car back from that angle (to open your jib leech); if you are looking for more power, go forward of that mark (to close or tighten the jib leech).

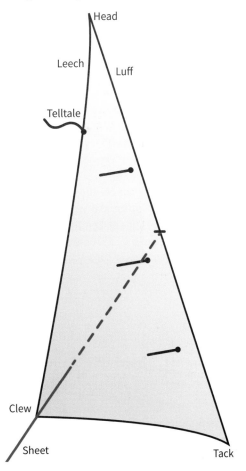

2. A telltale on the jib leech, a hand width underneath the top batten, or if you have no batten, about a quarter of the way down the leech is a sail-tuning must. This telltale shows the flow of air on the exit of your sail. If it is flying horizontally you have flow, if it is curling behind the jib the wind is stalling.

A telltale on the jib leech is a sail-tuning must

3. Foredeck marks give you a visual aid as to the depth of your jib. If you are new to the boat, figuring out the right place for this can be hard. My best advice is go and have a look at someone who is fast and copy what they have! If that isn't an option, thread some twine through the bottom forestay fixing point to the shroud and mark a 10cm line where the middle of the jib foot would sit. In the 470 you would make 2 further parallel lines at 5cm intervals towards the gunwale, but the exact measurements may differ for other classes – ask your sailmaker.

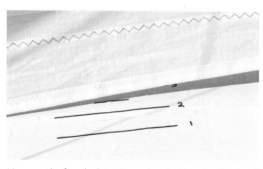

Lines on the foredeck to give a visual aid to the depth of the jib

4. Put a mark on the jibsheet and some calibration marks on the deck that the jibsheet runs past. This is just for a quick visual reference, out of manoeuvres, that you are near the right place.

Mark your jibsheet and put calibration marks on the deck

In simplistic terms:
- A deep jib with a tight leech adds power, until you go too far.
- A flat jib is less powerful but creates an easy shape for light wind to travel across, again until you go too far.
- An open leech gets rid of power.

These visual aids will show you what you need to do with the jib, but you need to decide how to achieve it: with jibsheet or jib car? For example, if the leech telltale is wrapped around the back of the sail, you need to open the jib:
- You need to ease more jibsheet out to get the telltale flying more but, as you do that, you are losing drive from your jib (the front starts caving slightly), as it is just too far out on the sheet.
- So, go forward on your car setting, which makes your leech tighter, but ease the jibsheet to get the telltale flying.
- So, the base of your jib is still pulling, but you have opened up the top.

When you are on the water consider the wind strength, sea state and the feeling in the boat when sailing in a straight line and discuss what you need from your jib:

- Is it light, sitting-in-the-boat conditions? If so, you need to encourage flow over your jib and onto your mainsail = LOOKING FOR POWER
- Is it hiking / trapezing conditions and there is room for the boat to take more wind before you would be over powered? If so, you are looking to squeeze as much wind as possible onto the mainsail = LOOKING FOR POWER
- Are you already completely overpowered? If so, you need to lose wind from the mainsail = LOOKING TO LOSE POWER
- Is there a chop / wave that you are smashing into? If so, you need a forgiving jib set-up that will cover a few bases: sometimes you need power, other times you need to get rid of it = BIT OF EVERYTHING.

Light Wind

In the lighter wind you need to have a more 'open' jib leech to encourage the weak, less powerful air across your jib, through the slot. Have the leech telltale flying 80% of the time, stalling 20%. As the wind builds you can increase the amount of time it is stalling.

Building To Max Power

As the wind builds, it has more energy and can push through that gap more easily, so you need to tighten your jib leech, maximising the power you can take out of the wind. As you hit the toestraps or the trapeze wire the jib can take a significant pull in. Have the leech telltale stalling 80% of the time and flowing 20%. This will be a gradual tightening all the way up to max power, when your jib leech will be at its tightest. If your jib leech telltale is constantly flying, your jib leech is too open; if it is constantly wrapped around the leech of the sail, your jib is too tight.

Beyond Max Power

When you get beyond max power, you now need to start losing (spilling) wind from your sail, because your body weight can no longer balance it out, so you start opening the leech again. The leech telltale becomes less useful in these conditions as it will permanently fly, unless you are over tight. Instead look at the luff of the mainsail. If you are sailing upwind in a straight line and the mainsail luff is constantly back-winding, it is being caused by wind firing off the back of jib into the luff of the mainsail and it's not fast. You want both sails to be pulling together, not one disrupting the airflow over the other. So, ease the sheet until you are back-winding 20% of the time.

Sailing beyond max power   © Thom Touw

Chop

I think choppy conditions are the hardest to set up for: what you need from your jib is constantly changing, you need power to punch through the difficult water and, if you hit a bad wave and the boat starts loading up, you need to quickly get rid of that power and encourage flow so you can accelerate. In these conditions you would set your jib up at it's most 'twisted': with a deep base that gives you the power, but an open top leech to give you the forgiveness so, if you keep hitting waves, you can re-accelerate. So, it would be jib car forward, jibsheet eased.

Essentially the correct jib set-up is a blend of both jib car and sheeting position. It's not an exact science and has a large element of personal preference and feel to it. Also, the boat is always in transition from one state to another, so you have to be fully on top of what is coming on to your boat and sails next and what you need to change the set up to. I've vastly over simplified it here, so would encourage you to understand it deeper by reading the *Tuning to Win* book in the *Sail to Win* series.

Technique Practice

The next element of speed is your technique both individually and how you work together. It's hugely boat, wind speed and wave state specific. The two main elements are boat heel (side-to-side) and boat trim (front-to-back).

Sailing in a straight line you need to be looking at the wind that will be hitting your boat in the next 20 seconds and anticipating what you need to do with your body position and jibsheet position to maintain maximum speed.

Boat Heel

As a general rule across boats, when it's light wind you want leeward heel: this helps the helmsperson steer as it gives them weight through the tiller. As soon as the wind builds, and you get some boatspeed on, you feel like you can squeeze some power on and the boat needs to be flat. From this wind speed through to max power and up the wind range most boats will want to be flat. If you are in a planing boat, they like to sit on their planing surface upwind, which could well be flat but, depending on design, it might be with a few degrees of leeward heel.

Most of the boat heel work is the crew's job, but there might be a few conditions where, as a team, you feel it is more accurate and less disruptive to the boat and sails if the helm takes charge of it. For my team this was 'crew in the boat conditions' when I was wedged down in a tight ball between the gunwale and side deck. The helm could control flattening the boat in the early stages of the building wind.

In the condition where you are just thinking to commit to the trapeze or the toestraps, it can be worth both helm and crew gently hiking until the wind is solidly established. That stops any disruption to the mast as you hook on and off if the windspeed fluctuates and sometimes drops down.

At max power, as a team, you are desperate to

As you move to max power, do everything you can to increase leverage

not be the first boat in the race to start giving away power, either by having to dump some mainsheet or depower the sail by pulling on kicker, so you need to do everything you can to increase your leverage. Trapezing or hiking off your tiptoes, your front arm over the head, getting your clothing wet so you weigh a bit more, anything so you can keep holding the power.

Whatever the situation requires heel wise, you want don't to be yo-yoing around between flat and heeled. As you can imagine, that disturbs the wind and water flow around your boat and isn't fast. If you are struggling to keep it dead flat, have a bit of heel on and aim to keep that consistent.

Boat Trim

Boat trim wise, if it's light winds, move your body weight as a team as far forward as possible to get the wide transom of your boat, which you are dragging around, out of the water. But you can go too far forward so, if it sounds and feels like you are ploughing through the ocean, then that's too far!

As the wind builds you want the maximum waterline length from your boat as that will get it up to maximum speed. So, as a team, spread out a bit, your crewing position will start off near the shrouds and, as the wind builds more, move further back to the widest part of the boat, where you have maximum leverage. There will be little bits of chop or wave to move forwards or backwards on, whichever feels the right thing: this will help the boat keep smooth and not bounce around.

As you move into planing mode you need to move back to 'pop' or free the bow out of the water so you don't plough into the waves. It also puts the boat onto its planing surface, which is the most efficient for speed.

A huge element of performance is how you transition through these modes as the wind builds or drops. If you are planing in a gust with weight back but about to enter a lighter patch, it is hugely important not to waste any time in moving forward and sheeting your jib harder so the helm can instantly head up, transitioning to displacement sailing and vice versa if you are trying to plane.

In a fast asymmetric trapeze dinghy, the trapezing position moves aft once it is windy enough to plane upwind: by about 70cm in an RS800 for example. You should see the knuckle of the bow lift out the water when the sea is flat. The decision on when to trim back should be made by the person who is sheeting the main because they can feel when the boat is ready to plane.

Up & downwind (but particularly upwind): If trapezing in a double trapeze boat, keeping both helm and crew bodies at same height and close together reduces windage which is important for speed in windy conditions for a boat driven by apparent wind.

Communicate with the helm to agree your trapezing height and fore & aft trim.

Body Weight

The final upwind technique element is how you can use your body weight to flick the leech (back part) of the mainsail, called bouncing or pumping, which accelerates wind off the back of the sail. This is controlled by Rule 42 so is prohibited upwind unless your class rules create an exception, which increasingly classes are doing at a certain wind strength.

The outcome you are trying to achieve is movement in the mast, which then affects the sail. It is easy to feel a jolt through the boat that doesn't translate to any effect on the sail. If you are trapezing this will be a fast jolt downwards with the hips, so the energy goes straight up the wire. It is not a flick through the feet or ankles. Use this technique when you are over powered and need to exhaust some wind out of the sail, so at the top of a wave or as a gust hits to get you back to upright.

This unprohibited pumping is also being increasingly used in under max power conditions: the flag to allow it has to be hoisted (Flag O). In this situation it is not being used to exhaust wind out of the sail but to increase the power and go faster. You are trying to repeatedly replicate the pull down out of a roll tack and essentially row yourself faster through the wind.

Give the boat a little leeward heel and then

pull down through the trapeze wire to vertical: rhythmically repeat this process and you will feel that, as the boat gains speed, you will be able to build the force and speed that you can pull through the wire. The technique and application of this style of pumping are constantly evolving so if it's happening in your class, watch and speak to the experts to understand how and when to use it.

Downwind Speed

I've written this section focussing on a symmetric spinnaker boat but obviously much of what is written here is also relevant for non-spinnaker and asymmetric spinnaker boats. At the end, Rob and Emma provide a few additional pointers for asymmetric spinnaker boats.

Once the spinnaker is hoisted and the pole is clipped on, settle on the windward side of the boat so you have a clear view of the spinnaker luff: the edge of the spinnaker nearest to you.

- Start with pulling the guy back with your front hand so the pole is at 90° to the wind direction (this is a good reason to have a burgee or wind indicator at the top of the mast).
- Cleat the guy in that position.
- Next trim the spinnaker sheet so the spinnaker stops flapping.
- Gently ease the spinnaker sheet out so the spinnaker luff starts curling and then pull it so that curling just stops.
- Constantly check with a small ease that you are always very close to the spinnaker luff curling.
- Keep checking that your spinnaker pole is still at 90° to the wind. As you go faster and the apparent wind increases, the direction of the apparent wind will move forward, so you will need to move the pole forward and trim the sheet more.

Pole Height

Loads of people will say the right pole height is with both spinnaker clews (corners) horizontally level. I find that really hard to see and actually I'm sure sometimes it's not right, so get used to looking

at the shape of your spinnaker luff and understand what looks balanced. You want a nice even curve which, when you ease the sheet, the curl starts around the middle:

- If the pole is too high, the shape of the semi circle will be skewed so it is deeper at the top of the spinnaker and the luff will start breaking lower down the spinnaker.
- If the pole is too low, the curve the luff makes is too flat and there will be no depth and power in your sail.

Light Wind Trimming

When it's light you are desperate to get the spinnaker floating as far away from the forestay and mast as possible to allow more wind into the spinnaker. Initially this can be a bit of a tricky concept to achieve, because the obvious thing is to ease the spinnaker sheet but then there is a tendency to pull the guy around to stop it from flapping, but then you are sailing around with a poorly trimmed spinnaker. You need to try to float the whole spinnaker away from the boat, while keeping it square to the wind: so, you need to ease on both sheet and guy so the sail floats forward.

The lighter the wind becomes the harder it is to trim: drop the pole height which will give the spinnaker a bit of weight again and make it easier to fly. As soon as the wind builds, raise the pole height again to give your spinnaker depth and power.

As you improve you might uncleat the guy rope and keep the tension in your arm for quick and easy trimming. Although this is good for accurate guy position beware of losing any power through your arm as a gust comes on. If it's cleated the gust can transfer power straight into the spinnaker.

Heavy Wind Trimming

This is the opposite to light wind trim: the windier it becomes the more you want to strap the spinnaker close to the boat so it doesn't roll around and take charge of the steering. Tightening both sheet and guy towards the boat stretches the spinnaker out and flattens the shape so it is less powerful.

Flying the spinnaker in light winds

Boat Heel & Trim

There will be constant little adjustments to make in your body weight with all the fluctuations in wind. As general rule, in the lighter stuff you'll be sat right next to the shroud with your legs positioned so that you can move your weight inboard easily if the wind drops and you need to put leeward heel on. This might be with one or both legs to leeward of the centreboard case.

As the wind builds towards max power you need to be able to slide in during the lulls but also be in a position that you can spring out, pull the boat flat and get an acceleration if the wind builds. As it gets windier, and normally wavier, your body weight will move back to stop the bow of the boat digging in, and you will want to have a more stable locked-in position so that you don't get pushed around by the more aggressive steering or pull from your spinnaker sheet.

The light wind position with weight through your legs so you can push out or slide in

Advanced Speed

There are obviously strategic and tactical choices to make downwind but choosing the mode that works to get you downwind, towards your leeward mark, the fastest is a huge area for development and teamwork between helm and crew.

This is achieved two ways:

1. Sail a lower angle, which is a more direct route to the leeward marks but at a slower speed as, essentially, you are getting pushed by the wind so will only go as fast as the windspeed.
2. Sail a higher angle, which increases your apparent wind and therefore boatspeed, but you sail more distance. As a bonus, as you sail faster, your apparent wind increases and moves forward, which means that you can then bear away and sail a lower, more direct route.

This is called VMG (velocity made good) meaning it is a balance between having good speed and going in a good direction. In a conventional spinnaker boat and a boat with no spinnaker the fastest way downwind will involve a mixture of these 2 techniques, which will be highly dependent on windspeed and wave angle.

Your role will be to understand how much pressure in the kite is too little or too much and get your helm to steer the boat higher or lower based on this.

Get used to the feel of pressure in the spinnaker through the spinnaker sheet – you might want to use thinner spinnaker sheets so that you have a more sensitive feel, because your feedback on this puts you in control of where the helm steers the boat. If you feel pressure through your hand, feel that your speed has built, and you can sail the boat at a deeper angle without the speed dropping too much, call that to your helm and, if there is some leeward heel, flatten the boat to help the steer down. Conversely if you feel you are too slow, and the sailing angle is too low, call to your helm to head up and help by putting a bit of leeward roll on the boat.

With the fluctuations in the windspeed the best mode (VMG) will change, so you will be constantly re-evaluating what you are feeling through the spinnaker and adjusting what you are doing. When you can't see any other boats it's easy to lose your calibration for speed and, as it feels nicer to have pressure in the kite, it's easy to sail too high. Conversely, if you can see boats in front of you (especially if you are close to gybing) it feels good to sail low and prevent them from gybing but actually you are too slow, so they will be able to gybe and cross anyway. Make sure you are honest with what you are feeling through your hand and not manipulating it for a perceived tactical scenario. Get your helm to give you input and feedback about how you are doing on other boats.

There might be tactical reasons that the helm is sailing high (to clear your lane) or low (to drop round someone's bow) but good communication between the team on what you are trying to achieve, and what you have the speed and pressure to do, is vital.

Waves

If there are waves to catch, in a simple scenario the waves will be travelling directly downwind. If you are lucky, how you are lined up on your downwind might be the right angle to get a surf on the wave, but you might also find that the boat surges briefly and the wave travels quickly through underneath you and you drop off the back of it and have to wait for the next one. If this is the case, you need to increase your boatspeed as the wave is travelling up underneath your transom:

*   Roll the boat to leeward, which will steer the boat up to angle without using rudder (which creates drag and slows the boat).
*   At this higher angle the apparent wind will increase and so will the boatspeed.
*   Pump the spinnaker – which means a SHARP pull or pulls of the spinnaker to scoop wind and accelerate the boat forwards. The speed and force that you pump with will totally depend on the wind strength. If the wind is solid then do a sharp, positive pump which squeezes the wind. If the wind is lighter you don't want to just pump the wind out of the kite and collapse

the spinnaker, so do a slower scoopy squeeze. Under Rule 42, you are restricted to one pump per wave, so the timing on the wave is vital for maximum impact. It will be as the boat is up to speed and just as you are preparing to flatten and the helm steers down the wave.

- Finally, to get the final bit of acceleration and as the wave is about mid ship, flatten the boat off with your body weight as the helm bears away and surf the wave downwind.
- So the order is ROLL, STEER, APPARENT (let the speed build), PUMP, FLATTEN. (I had 'RSAPF' written on my boat for years!)

There will be lots of things that influence whether you can get on the wave, how much speed you can get out of it and how long you can ride it for.

The class rules might allow for the pumping element of Rule 42 to get cancelled, so you are allowed to do multiple pumps per wave. It's still really important that these are well used and timed, and it doesn't just become a flap off. The speed building phase of the sequence is when you can do multiple pumps to increase your boatspeed further. Make sure to use your arms on the pumps: if you use your back you might inadvertently flatten the boat slightly and not have any heel left to do the final powerful flatten.

If you are planing on the wave and starting to decelerate there could be the opportunity for another pump on the spinnaker to keep you surfing a bit longer. If Rule 42 is still applied, you need to be really strict with yourself that you don't break the rule here with an extra pump, but also it might not be the right decision speed wise. It's possible that you have got the best out of that wave and it's time to set up for the next one. Too many teams get too low and slow on what was a good wave, but it means it takes them too long to set up for the next wave behind and they miss it. Make sure that you keep a monitor on how many waves you are missing: it could mean you are riding them too long.

Make sure that you don't pump the spinnaker round to windward. Your guy arm will be directly

'1 to 1', meaning that the distance your arm travels will be the distance your spinnaker moves. Depending on your boat and how your spinnaker sheet is rigged, the sheet could be '1 to 1' or '2 to 1' – in the latter case, for the sheet to move the same distance as the guy, your sheet arm needs to be pulled twice the distance of the guy arm. You are trying to pump the spinnaker evenly towards the boat in its trimmed position, not rotate it as you do it, so it is important that both sides of the spinnaker move the same amount, otherwise you will lose power.

Be aware that there will be times when the waves are just moving too fast for you to get on them. However hard you pump you just can't get your boat up to a 'take off speed'. Tell-tale signs of this will be that you keep calling to sail higher to increase the apparent wind, but you never manage to do a flatten and get on the wave. In these conditions one option is to sit at the correct VMG and get the occasional surf rather than to keep sailing high. There might be the odd wave to pop it high and try to get on, or you could try to sail across the wave at a low angle, by the lee, and gain downwind VMG.

There are also days when the wave is actually really slow and doesn't have a lot of energy to give you. It's really tempting to push out a low slow VMG and gain depth to the marks. There will be times when this is the right option and occasionally there might be a bigger, powerful wave that rolls down that you can get going forwards on. Alternatively see below for the wild thing!

There will definitely be days when the wave won't be square to your downwind course. One downwind tack might be perfectly set up for the downwind surfing angle ('the fast gybe') and the other you will be sailing across the wave.

The fast gybe is straightforward and lovely as you will be perfectly lined up on the downwind angle to sail a few degrees higher, build some speed, with or without a pump, accelerate and surf.

There are two ways to deal with the slow gybe. Your first option might be to sail it high and fast, just so that you get it done quickly – the extra distance you sail should be offset by doing it slightly faster and getting back onto and giving yourself more time on the fast gybe. Alternatively, it might be possible to surf the wave low, by the lee, and get depth on the wave.

The speed waves are travelling, their angle, your strategic options and the tactical battles you are in will determine how and why you choose what technique will be the best for you in each particular circumstance. Be flexible on what style you are choosing: the run might be made up of a mixture of all of them. Be honest if you think it is not working.

When It All Feels Wrong

One of the worst feelings downwind is if you feel you are digging yourself into a hole. This often happens if both helm and crew are working really hard to get on the wave but haven't quite got the order and tempo right between them. For example, there is no point in pumping unless you are at the right angle to the wave.

To build the right tempo between you, start with roll (leeward heel on the boat) which will help with steering the boat up (to get you to the right angle), wait for the apparent wind to build and

finally pump (the sails and the boat flat).

Wild Thing!!

There are times when the waves are moving slow and the boat gets stuck in that one wave, but you feel there is enough wind that you should be overtaking the wave or there is a really steep chop / awkward wave that's impossible to sail through. This is the moment to wild thing and it's really fun!

Basically, you sail a high, fast mode with the crew on the wire, standing medium back on the boat trim; the helm will stay on the leeward tank. Stay high on your trapeze wire because you still want to sail as low as possible and you'll need your feet a bit further apart than normal as you will accelerate and decelerate quite fast.

There might be times that you do the whole downwind wild, and other times when you just pop it into that mode for a section, to get through some bad sea state or get some separation away from some other boats quickly. It's really important to monitor if it's working, as you have to have increased your boatspeed enough to justify sailing the extra distance. It's an important technique to practise as it can create a huge opportunity for gain.

Preparing to go out on the trapeze to go wild

Additional Pointers for Asymmetrics

Asymmetric boats tend to share the same upwind fundamentals as Saskia explains, but downwind is a different art.

Downwind, the helm really relies on the crew to find the lowest and fastest course to the leeward mark. The crew's key roles are to trim the spinnaker perfectly and move their weight to maximise speed.

There are three basic modes for downwind asymmetric sailing. In all modes it is essential that you are easing the kite to keep the luff on the point of curling at all times. Not only is this fastest, but it is also the helm's guide to the apparent wind angle. You should agree when you are changing mode.

1. Light Winds = 'Soak mode'
In non-planing winds, the aim is to sail as low as you can without the kite collapsing.

Your position will generally be fairly static downwind. The general aim is to keep weight forward and in a position where you can see the luff of the spinnaker at all times. In the RS200, I like to kneel in the middle of the boat (one knee either side of the centreboard case) so that I can peer around the mast / forestay at the luff. Pressing my weight onto one knee or the other is generally sufficient.

In a trapeze skiff like an RS800, you will need to be in front of the mast for correct trim of the boat. You will be sat as far forward as possible in the lightest breeze, edging back as the wind builds. Ideally sit just far enough out on the side so that you can see the kite to keep it perfectly trimmed. Boats that can angle the pole to windward (like the 4000) will have it angled back.

The perfectly trimmed asymmetric is just on the edge of having the luff of the spinnaker curling, which is impossible to achieve in reality. Therefore, easing the sheet so the luff curls the smallest amount possible before needing a little sheet on to correct requires constant attention. All the while, the crew constantly tells the helm how low

they can go – if the sheet starts to lose pull in your hand, this means that the sail is about to collapse, and the boat is being sailed on too low an angle. As soon as this starts to happen, a simple verbal note to the helm will prompt them to luff and power things up again. Similarly, when the sheet feels a little heavier than it should for the wind strength, it may be time for the helm to bear away.

At times it can be difficult to feel the power in the spinnaker through the sheet – the weight of the line and friction in the hardware override any pull. Another clue to feed back to the helm is what the spinnaker looks like. If the luff disappears around the forestay but remains full: bear away; while if the sail forms to windward more than you are used to seeing, it might be time to bear away. Ideally the spinnaker is stably 'bubbling' around the forestay and responding well to your trim.

2. Marginal Planing Winds
Where subtlety meets activity. In these conditions, the crew's feedback to the helm is just as critical as in light winds. A conversation with the helm prior to rounding the windward mark will gauge the wind strength and the first 'mode' that will be sailed downwind.

When sailing downwind, a critical skill of the crew is the feel in the boat: being able to transition between soak mode and an effective low-planing mode in a seamless way makes finding the quickest route downwind very easy.

When low planing in the RS200, I like to squat 'in the box' behind the thwart (without getting in the way of the mainsheet) and press any gusts down by pressing my back against the side deck before returning to the box while the helm rides the pressure downwind.

In a trapezing asymmetric, as soon as the boat can plane, the crew moves back and out onto the wire. The helm heads up until the luff of the kite is vertical. In a 4000 the pole is cleated on the centreline. Wire high as you are not aiming for maximum righting moment in this mode; the helm will be sat in the boat. The crew should move forward in the lulls and aft in the gusts.

3. Windy 'Send It'

In this mode, there is a trade-off between out and out speed and gaining depth to leeward. Although exhilarating and hard work, these conditions are generally easier to sail quickly downwind in than marginal planing. The plan is simple: Luff in the lulls and bear away in the gusts. The crew can assist the helm's steering with hiking when the gusts hit and moving inboard in the lulls.

Keeping the luff curling occasionally is still key, however make sure to give the sheet an ease when a gust initially hits. This will allow the sail to absorb the new pressure without pulling the rig sideways. Once this flow is established and the boat accelerates, the apparent wind will go forwards and you will need to sheet in.

With a trapeze, the helm starts wiring or hiking hard and bears away more and more as the wind builds. You are aiming for maximum righting moment so wire low and move right back in the boat. If it is rough, use the footloop at the back of the boat to stop you falling forward if the boat hits a wave. Be prepared when a gust hits to ease the kite sheet immediately as the apparent wind comes aft and the helm bears away to keep the boat level.

In steep waves, if there is a risk of the boat nose diving into the wave in front, over-sheeting the kite sharply with a big armful of sheet will control the speed and lift the bow. This is a very effective way to save yourselves from pitchpoling but ease the sheet as soon as it is safe to minimise loss of boatspeed.

Over-sheeting the kite to depower is also useful when you are on port approaching a starboard gybe boat and want to pass behind them rather than be forced to gybe. In this case you may need to pull in several armfuls of sheet to sufficiently slow the boat. Agree first with your helm that this is the plan!

Throughout the wind ranges, we are constantly trying to maximise the surfing effect of the waves. Even in light winds, a small push forwards with your weight as the water drops away from the bow will push the boat down the face of a wave, however, make sure to move back again before you crash into the next. 'Playing the waves' takes a lot of refinement and coordination with the helm (steering and pumping), so get out there, have a play and establish what works best. I found that going sailing against the best downwind sailing team at the club for a session out at sea was the quickest way to learn the effort and techniques in all conditions.

Reaching

When reaching, ideally you would go at maximum speed in a straight line to the next buoy, but this plan is often disrupted by the presence of other boats. I therefore cover reaching speed in the racing section – see p117.

At some point you will inevitably capsize. With a bit of practise it doesn't have to be a total race-ending disaster and you'll be able to make quick recovery.

Firstly, put every bit of effort into stopping it happening, hike hard and bounce at the critical point of when your boom end hits the water. If you are trapezing try to unhook without falling into the sail and, with two hands on the trapeze handle, get your centre of gravity low and bounce as much as you can to try keeping the boat upright.

Once it's definitely gone, quickly get to your action stations. If it's gone turtle, you will probably both be needed on the centreboard to get it halfway up. Be really aware of whether you have hit the bottom with your mast. If you have, don't put your weight on the hull of the boat as that could result in a broken or bent mast. If you think the mast has hit the bottom, try to lever it upright from the side, with your weight on the lowest gunwale.

As soon as the boat is half up, one of you can get on the centreboard and the other will go and sort the spinnaker if it is up. In my team the lighter person stayed on the centreboard as she was big enough, especially if there was wind helping her, to right the boat, and I did the swimming around as being heavier helped later on in the process.

Depending how windy it is, you might get away with keeping the spinnaker up, but if it's quite windy it will pull too much and stop you righting the boat. Swim round to the inside of the boat, uncleat the kicker and the spinnaker halyard if it needs to come down, as the person on the centreboard pulls the spinnaker sheet nearest them to get the spinnaker down as low as possible, but importantly lower than the shrouds, as quickly as possible. If they can stuff any of it in a spinnaker

Try to do everything in your power to stay upright

bag that is a bonus. With a spinnaker chute, pull the spinnaker into the chute.

It's important to get to this stage as quickly as possible after capsizing to hopefully avoid getting the spinnaker wrapped around the spreaders. The person in the water then swims to the front of the boat, holds the forestay fitting and tries to swim the boat head to wind as much as possible, when that is done the person on the centreboard rights the boat.

If it's really windy the boat will blow round so that the mast is pointing into the wind and, when you pull it upright, it will immediately roll into another capsize. In this case, instead of going to the forestay fitting, swim to the shroud that is in the water, put your feet on the deck either side of the shroud, hold onto the shroud at shoulder height and float as if you were standing on the side deck. Let the buoyancy aid take your weight, so you are not pulling the boat back into a turtle capsize. When you are ready call for the boat to be righted and you will pop up on the windward side, standing by the shroud and hopefully will prevent it rolling straight over again. Quickly climb backwards and get the tiller.

In both scenarios, get someone to the tiller to steer the boat up into wind and get some control back. Then help the other person into the boat. If you need to, swap round so you are in the right place and sort out the mess! In boats where the helm is significantly smaller, it can be a good idea for them to sort the mess, especially if some of it is down to leeward as it keeps most of the crew weight up to windward.

Sometimes the inevitable happens

RACING

© Thom Touw

PART 3

CHAPTER 12

Introduction To Racing

So now the fun bit! I love racing but, if you are new to it, it can be a daunting prospect. Remember that everyone went through that phase and actually, as you continue to improve and race at a higher level, the feeling can stay for a long time! Don't be shy to ask more experienced sailors questions to improve your technique or racing skills – the sailing community is generally very friendly and inclusive.

You may have teamed up with someone who has a lot more experience than you but, as you continue on your journey, take ownership of roles that make sense, so that you can grow into a crewing role.

I've tried to break this section down into the various roles that fall into a crew's remit, but people are naturally better or worse at certain things, so it might be that in your team it works better if you switch it around. That is all part of the process of being a good team: playing to your strengths, while discussing and improving your weaknesses.

How A Race Works

In the Sailing Instructions or Notice of Race, there will be a published start time. Depending on what event you are doing they might also prescribe the course to be sailed in that document or, if you are doing some club racing, it will more likely be posted at the clubhouse when you are getting ready to launch or on the committee boat at the start.

The race committee will get the start line and course set up and will indicate (probably with an orange flag) to standby for the start countdown.

The start line will be an imaginary line between a mast on the start boat and a buoy / mast at the other end of the line. If you are club racing it could be a transit start line as shown in the diagram. For the best start, you need to be just behind the line, heading at your racing angle at maximum speed on the start signal.

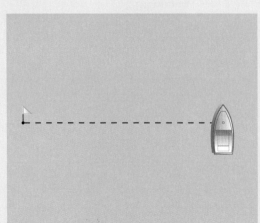

Committee boat starting line

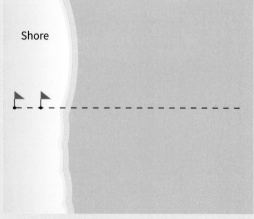

Club transit start line

The Start Sequence

The standard start sequence is as follows, although different clubs and different events may have a different format:

- At 5 minutes to go, a sound signal will be made, and a class flag will be hoisted. If it's only one fleet racing this will be your 5-minute signal, if there are multiple classes then check if this is your start (your class flag will be stated in the Sailing Instructions).
- The course must be displayed by the 4-minute signal, so sail past the committee boat and check.
- At 4 minutes to go, there is another sound signal with flag P.

- At 1 minute to go, flag P will come down with a sound signal.

Flag P (the Preparatory signal)

- On the go, the class flag is removed with a sound signal.

If any boats were over the start line at the starting signal:

- If the race committee can identify them all, they will hoist flag X with an additional sound signal, which means that all the boats who were over the line can return behind the line, restart and race on.

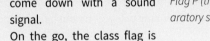

Flag X

- If they can't identify them all, and especially if it was a significant amount of the fleet, they will hoist the 1st substitute flag with 2 additional sound signals. This is a general recall and you'll go back to the 5-minute signal shortly (or at the end of the sequence if there are multiple starts).

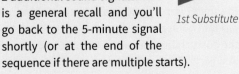

1st Substitute

At the 4-minute signal, instead of flag P, the committee can choose to display a number of other flags. These are the most likely:

- **Flag I**: If you are over the start line in the final minute countdown you have to return to the pre-start side of the start line by going around an end of the line to have a valid start.

Flag I

- **Flag U**: If you are over the start line in the final minute before the start you will be disqualified from the race, but you can re-join the race if there is a general recall.

Flag U

- **Black flag**: If you are over the start line in the final minute before the start you will be disqualified from the race, even if there is a general recall or the race is abandoned but re-sailed.

Black flag

Race Day

There will be a published time for the start, so work back from that to get your launching and meeting time. Think about:

- How much preparation time do you want on the water pre-start?
- How long it will take you to sail / tow to the start area?
- Will there be a queue on the slipway / launching ramp?
- How long do you need to set up the boat and get changed?

Considering all of that, it might be that you meet at the boat 2-3 hours before start time. Pre-arrange who is dealing with snacks and drinks, or if you are looking after yourselves individually.

Run through all the settings you might use for the day's racing, checking that your boat is marked up so you know how to get to them on the water. (Advice on settings can be found in *Tuning to Win*, also part of the *Sail to Win* series.)

It's worth recording this so, if you have a blistering day on the water, you know what your static settings were and can replicate them another time. Likewise, if you don't feel fast on the water, you can go back and check to see where the problem might have been.

CHAPTER 13

Pre-Start

Whether you are going out for a championship day or a Wednesday evening club race, it's always good to turn up in the starting area with a little bit of time to spare. Detailed below is the process I use for a race day at a World Cup event. How much weighting and time you give each element will obviously depend on how much time you have and how important the event is to your team.

Boat Set-Up

As you arrive at the race area go straight into an upwind tuning session to identify if you are on the right mast rake settings. Remember there might still be significant time to the start and the conditions have a long time to change, especially if you are in a sea breeze venue. So, if you feel like you are near a transition zone, don't waste too much time making a decision at this point.

Jib Set-Up

Give yourselves a bit of time just to settle into the conditions. If you are a trapeze crew, get your trapeze height in the right range. Get your jib leech in the right place. Think about the strength of the wind and the sea state and what this means in relation to how tight you want your jib leech, and how much jibsheet or jib car you might need to be moving in the varying wind or wave conditions.

Technique Practice

Think about the wind conditions you are in and, from a boatspeed perspective, where the gains will come from:

- Is it a light / medium wind, flat water day, where holding a lane is going to be vital, so a high emphasis is on accuracy of sheet position and crew weight?
- Is the wind strength in that transition phase

from displacement to planing (obviously if you are in a planing boat!) so getting the crew weight back and popping the jibsheet an inch at the crucial time will get you pushing forward fast?

- Is it top end wind conditions, where the losses will come from screwing up into the wind and flapping sideways until you can get control back? So, practise your pre-emptive strategy of a big jib ease and a step forward to maximum leverage position.

The discussion around these things will inform how you set up your boat and whether you need to lose or find power. It will get your team on the same wavelength, talking the same language with the same objective.

As well as the upwind set-up, get the range of the shifts (on your compass if you use one) and a sense of how quickly the wind is moving through the shift range. Can you identify any pattern to the shifts? Is it a 10-degree range over 10 minutes, random 20-degree shifts moving very fast? Are all the gusts shifting one way? Or is it totally random? (As Nick Craig emphasises in *Tactics to Win*, knowing it is random is useful input and far better than convincing yourself there is a pattern when there isn't!)

When you are happy with your upwind set-up, if you have a symmetric spinnaker, hoist onto what would be an appropriate top reach angle, so you know where to pull your twinners or guy back to (depending on what system you are using).

After a short reach, bear away on to a run. It's really easy to waste this bit of the downwind, discussing what you have learnt on the upwind and potential race strategy, but use the downwind for technique. Find the right rhythm between you both on the weight distribution for steering the boat, the right tempo on the rocking and pump, and the right work rate. Bear in mind that the water might be extra flat right now as boats and RIBs haven't sailed through it and chopped it up. Do a few gybes to assess the amount of roll needed and speed of flatten on the exit.

If you have an asymmetric spinnaker, ensure that you've completed at least one hoist, gybe and drop to check that the kite is rigged correctly and to assess the wind and wave conditions downwind. If you have time to sail to the windward mark you will be able to check whether the kite can be held on the spreader reach or not (if there is a spreader mark).

If you have a dagger board, take note if there is any weed in the water and plan a pre-start lift of the board to clear any weed you might have picked up before the race starts.

Strategy Discussion

When you are happy with your downwind speed, start talking about your first upwind strategy with your helm. From what you learnt on the upwind tuning and the speed and frequency of the shifts, what will be important in the race? You could easily have a list of questions written down in the boat to promote the conversation:

- Will lanes, shifts, or pressure be the most important factor?
- Is the shift range so small that it makes it a boatspeed race?
- What is the tide doing right now and what is it due to do over the duration of the race? How will that affect your strategy?
- Is any land mass affecting the race course?
- Is the wind forecast predicting anything that

could have an effect?
- Are the clouds giving us any information right now?

It's important that this discussion has actionable output that leads to decisions on strategy like where you want to start and if you think there is a favoured side of the course, rather than just a load of answers that lead to no strategic decisions.

For example, if you've discussed that it's a fast-moving shift range coming down with pressure, what actions does that mean you will take for the start and the upwind? Will you give away line bias to be nearest the first bit of pressure and will you make a late call on that in the starting sequence? Regardless of bias, would you start on port and duck the fleet if it immediately put you on the right shift and pressure?

If there is any tide, mentally go around the whole course and verbally say what it will mean. For example, if the tide is going left to right as you look upwind, the implications might be:
- It will make it hard to start at the committee boat end.
- The pin end will open up and could have space late on.
- There will be a long starboard tack upwind.
- It will be easy to over lay on starboard layline upwind, so there is the potential to tack in late.
- There will be a long time on starboard downwind.
- You will be pushed onto leeward marks from the left.
- There will be a long top reach against the tide, and you could get pushed high / low depending on the exact angle.

Again, Nick Craig's *Tactics to Win* covers this in more detail.

107

Starting Drills

An output of your strategy discussion should be a decision on where you want to start, and it should be a start that complements your upwind strategy, not definitely one that would make it impossible.

If you've decided that holding out to the left of the course is vital, then a pin end start is the most preferable option. However, the pin end can often be a highly congested area, so you might consider starting in space further up the line, lessening the risk of starting in a congested area, executing a reasonable start to hold your lane and not get immediately bounced to the right. There will, of course, be races when the outcome is decided at the start and you have to be the boat that executes the start in a congested area in order to win, but this probably happens on fewer occasions than people think, and, in a series of races, it becomes less vital to be that boat.

Whatever your starting decision, it is worth doing a few warm up starts, especially when there is tide. Evaluate where you want to start, figure out where the layline is for that position, how much drift there is when you are downspeed and flapping, what the slowest speed is that you need to be moving for the amount of wind to keep grip on the foils; and do a few practice accelerations so you know how long it takes you to get from stationary to full speed.

Sail slowly and understand how much sideways drift you are experiencing

Understand how far you have to bear away to get the boat powered up

Lean the boat to leeward to help steer the boat up

Pull the boat flat and power over the line at full speed

When the start line is set, start getting your transits, but be aware that they can still move the line up to the preparatory (4 minute) signal. It's always tempting to not get enough transits far enough back, but 5 boat-lengths back at the starboard end is only 1 ¼ boat lengths when you are three quarters of the way down the line, which you definitely need. Beware if it is light winds or there is tide, you may not have enough time to get to the other end of the line to get transits and back to where you want to start in the time available – so prioritise what you need to get done.

Check the course board after the preparatory signal. If they have posted a windward mark bearing, pop the boat head to wind and understand if the beat has a long tack.

Get the line bias. There are a few ways to do line bias. My preferred way is to take a bearing down the line and add 90 degrees if you are at the boat end or subtract 90 degrees if you took it from the pin end. That number is what the line is set square to so, whenever you pop head to wind during the sequence to get the wind direction, you can quickly decide how much bias there is either way.

In the pre-start routine, keep an eye on what the wind is doing: is it trending one way, has the

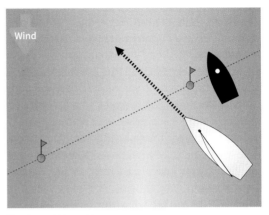

Starboard biased line

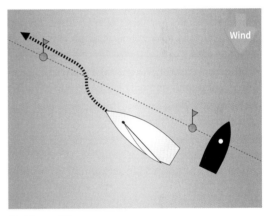

Port biased line

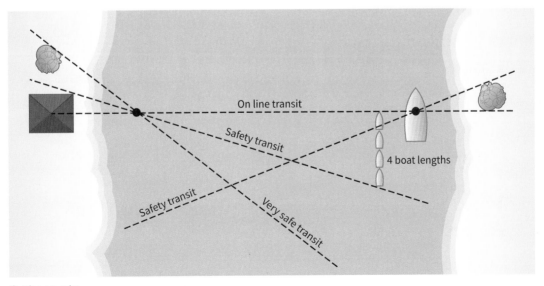

Getting transits

condition totally changed since you did your pre-start tune up and do you need to re-check that you are set up right? Does everything you discussed regarding strategy still hold true, are there any new elements to consider? Sometimes your previous strategy discussion will become totally irrelevant and you quickly have to reassess and make fresh decisions based on the new conditions. Most of the time it might just be a subtle adjustment to what you have already discussed or a reaffirming that your strategy is right. If there is tide, make sure that you never get too far away from where you need to be.

Throughout the pre-start keep popping the boat head to wind to check the wind direction and what this means for the line bias. Does it change what you have decided to do?

This pre-start routine will take up most of your preparatory time. Be really aware of the time you have left and be prepared to drop some of that routine if you need to save time.

All of this might feel like a lot to take on board, so if you are new to sailing and just developing your role: make your life easy. Write the compass number range on the deck so you remember it. If you keep forgetting stuff, write yourself reminders.

If you are transitioning from helming to crewing, it's important to commit to your new roles as a crew and not repeat jobs that you might previously had as a helm. Between you and your helm you need to assign roles based on your strengths and develop areas that you are weak on.

Throughout the pre-start it's the crew's job to call the time: every 10 seconds or so, in the 5- to 3-minute phase. As you get near 2 minutes to go you need to start thinking about your final approach. Now is the time have good communication about bunches of boats and where the space and lanes are if you decide to dip around behind them. At 2 minutes you should have time to establish yourself in a lane on the other side of them, but in the final 1 ½ minutes it could be too late.

Pre-start routines are a vital preparation for the start

Roles

Standard final approach roles for the crew are:

- Time (have a watch mounted on the mast or somewhere convenient that you can both see).
- Distance to line (hopefully with transits).
- Other boats that might attack your gap (you may allocate roles, so the crew has boats coming from the starboard end, helm the port end, or vice versa).
- Where there is space (important if you are losing your gap and need to bail out).
- Phase of wind (important because it alters your sailing distance and therefore time to the line and might influence your upwind strategy).
- Are you covered by other boats (can the committee boats see your sail number)?
- The 'trigger pull' (when to start your acceleration).

The helm has a lot on in the final approach, positioning the boat and defending your gap, and at points will be totally absorbed in doing that, so you might have to repeat a lot of information.

Communication

As with a lot of things in racing, good execution comes down to good communication. Above are the important jobs that you need to allocate, Most of the roles are for the crew as the helm will be absorbed by a lot of the technique around positioning the boat, but it might be different for each team. Cycle through the information at different times through the 5-minute countdown – the priority of certain bits will change.

Execution

Getting a good start doesn't guarantee a great race but it definitely makes it easier, so put the time in your training to practise the boat handling so that you can keep your gap to leeward and execute a great trigger pull whatever the wind and wave state. The specific skills will be boat dependent and require a lot of multi-tasking as you listen to what the helm needs you to do with the jib, in terms of backing it one side or the other to help them steer and also keep up with all your other jobs.

If your start is disastrous, there is not much to do but clear straight out. But there can be occasions where you didn't quite nail it but it's possible to survive in the lane for a bit. This could be a good option for a few reasons: all the people that got a really bad start will already have cleared out, so you will instantly have to duck fewer starboard boats. As a result of that, some starboard lanes might have opened up and you could get back onto starboard sooner than you think.

Equally there are other times when a quick clear out and big duck of the fleet is the best option.

© Thom Touw

CHAPTER 15

Upwind

Roles

The traditional view is that the crew makes decisions upwind while the helm is focussed on speed and vice versa for the downwind, but this is not always true or the right way for your team. Loads of modern boats have the crew trimming the mainsail, so their focus is on sail-set and speed; some conditions (e.g. light wind in a rolling swell) require huge concentration from the crew on balance to maintain top speed and with upwind pumping becoming more prevalent in some classes it's important to be flexible on who does what in various conditions. This approach also allows you to play to the individual strengths of your team.

I'd advocate having a good discussion about what is needed on the upwind and allocate the roles based on your strengths and weaknesses. Split the wind conditions into light, max power and heavy and have the discussion about roles again: things will change or go up or down the priority list.

Once you've allocated your roles it's really important to execute them on the water. If someone is butting into a role that isn't theirs, or a role is being missed, then information is either being duplicated or lost and important time is being wasted. It is very hard to debrief decision making and understand where things can be improved if no one has responsibility for it to begin with.

The key roles are:
- Speed
- Wind shifts
- Pressure

- Fleet positioning (on a big-picture scale: e.g. 30% are to the left of us)
- Course positioning (% time / distance left on each tack)
- Other boats (on a collision course with you)
- Lanes (that you can tack into)
- … and there might be more that you would add?

Decision Making

There are other *Sail to Win* titles that address tactics and decision making in a much more detailed way. Here I'm just going to describe the things that I think should be the tenants of your decision-making protocol and a process that are the beginnings of making you a good communicating, decision-making crew. Having a framework for how you make your decisions will make it easier to understand the mistakes you are making and where you can improve.

Different wind conditions bring different decision-making priorities: for example, a steady sea breeze day will be much more speed orientated and fleet biased than an offshore, gusty day, where you prioritise shifts and pressure over fleet positioning.

But a basic low-risk decision making framework would rotate through these 4 priorities, 3 of which are fact based and don't require any judgement:
- **Shift**: are we on mean or good compass numbers? If not, why not?
- **Fleet position**: are we in sync with the majority of the fleet, heading the same way as them? If not, why not?
- **Course position**: what is the long tack to the

mark right now? Do we need to be on it?

- **Pressure**: where is the best bit of pressure? Can we position ourselves for it?

A low-risk approach to decision making would mean that the first 3 of these would be right all the time. In reality it can never happen: you would constantly be tacking up the centre of the course to minimise the risk of a being on the short tack and you would be distinctly average. How these 3 things interact with each other, combined with positioning yourself well for the best pressure, is important. Every fleet and type of boat will have subtleties of how this works and it will also change through the wind range but as a basic rule:

If you are one-design racing and you are going against 2 of the first 3 things (shift, fleet, course) there needs to be a reason: don't do it accidentally.

That reason could be several things: holding on for a gust, holding on for a clear lane, you could be blocked from tacking by a starboard boat above you and the tack and duck is too big a loss – but, if you are going against shift, fleet position, or course, make it a conscious choice.

Being in the best wind pressure on the course is also key to winning races. Some days it is really easy to see the pressure and obvious what to do and other days it is much more subtle differences that end up having a big influence on the race. Unfortunately, I don't have any great answer for this except: get your eyes tested – it could make a big difference! And just keep trying to make the pressure observations and calls. But also, know that if you are finding it really difficult, it's likely that other teams are too.

When you are at the front of the fleet it's a bit easier to stay 'true' to always having 2 out of the first 3 right, as it's easier to stay in a clear lane, the next wind shift normally hits you first and you can choose where you tack.

As you go further back in the fleet it becomes harder and harder to tack exactly where you want to

on a shift because you are likely not to have a clear lane. It will be a balance of trying to make the best of it and inflicting the least damage. At these times it is really important to have a clear idea of your priorities and which one, for the conditions, will make the biggest impact. If it's fast moving shifts and you prioritise a clear lane, it will be impossible to ever sail a good shift – so prioritise sailing good numbers (compass heading) and don't worry too much about finding good lanes with clear air. It's impossible to outline the best scenario for every situation as a whole host of factors are at play but, if you are further back in the fleet, you need to re-evaluate the priorities and figure out which ones will help you overtake boats.

To start building your own playbook, identify at least 3 priorities for the different wind conditions. As an example, let's use an established but light (6-8kts) sea breeze day: the shift range is minimal, there are slight pressure differences over the course, the fleet tends to operate as a pack. Here are the priorities you might identify, the responsibilities and reasons for them:

- **Boatspeed**: As the shift range is small and creates little opportunity for overtaking, this kind of day is very boatspeed orientated, so make sure that you are confident on your set-up. Practise a few manoeuvres to make sure that you are putting enough energy into them, and gaining every inch around the course. **Both helm and crew are responsible**.
- **A good lane**: So you can execute good boatspeed. **Crew responsible**.
- **Execute a start to get a lane**: The start is a priority as the windshifts and pressure present little opportunity for overtaking, so get transits and line bias. Consider what you need to do about the line bias: do you need to take it and execute a start in the congested area of the line as it will be one of the few opportunities in the race; or would a bit of space away from the biased end, with less congestion and less risk, be a better option: you would have a good lane and can focus on speed. Starting away from the pin end could also give you an

immediate tack option if you are headed on starting. Your current overall position versus your expectation and the stage of the series will inform your choice. **Both helm and crew responsible**.

- **Sail the compass numbers**: Typically the wind is steady in this condition so being accurate on compass numbers and understanding what are high or low numbers is a priority to know if there is an opportunity on the shift. **Either responsible but allocate the role to one**.
- **Best pressure**: It is so important in this condition. **Either or both are responsible** but be aware of observations taking your focus away from speed especially in swell conditions.
- **Course & fleet position**: The fleet tends to operate as a big group. If you are not on the front row you need to pre-empt the momentum of the fleet with your position to tack so that you don't spend all the beat fighting for a clear lane. **Crew responsible**.

All the other elements of building an upwind leg will still be important, but these are identified as being priorities for this condition.

For some people this framework might seem over formalising something that should be fluid and dynamic. It's important when building a team, especially if you are coming with different levels of experience, that you start talking the same language and, in a given condition, are trying to achieve the same thing. Building a simplistic framework that achieves this will then create the headspace to observe and make dynamic race-winning decisions when there is the opportunity to do so.

If you are racing in a handicap (rather than one design) fleet it will influence how you interact with the fleet as you are also racing the clock. While the same principles apply in terms of exposing yourself to risk on the fleet and the course, it's important that you balance your focus on the fleet with what the right thing to do on the shift and course is. Consolidating on the fleet (tacking in sync with them to cover and track their movements) too much will give away precious time.

This process will get you some consistent results but potentially not winning races or series. As you build your playbook you will learn the times and conditions when you will be rewarded for exposing yourself to more risk. Understand the statistics of what it takes to win your series. In the 3 Olympics I competed at (10 race fleet series with 1 discard ending with 1 double points non-discardable medal race) an average place of 3.4 in the fleet racing element won the gold medal. This would be different in a 4-race series with no discard, and obviously different in a one-off race. Analysis like that will help you understand the average race result you need to get and how much risk you should expose yourself to getting it to achieve the outcome you want.

Speed

Tactics are undoubtedly easier if you are a fast boat, so it's worth the time and effort to become one. There will be certain conditions where, because of body weight or because you just really enjoy and are good in those conditions, that you are fast – but remember that, over a season or a campaign, the fleet can catch up, so it's important to still execute good decision-making procedure and understand if your gains or losses were speed related or because of your tactics or strategy.

All the observations and decision making in the world won't dig you out from being slow during a series of races so, during racing, devote enough time to accurately establishing your sail set-up and crew positioning. The sea and wind state will determine how much energy this will take away from your decision making but speed should always be high up the priority list. If you need to focus on speed so much that you are missing out on tactical and strategic observations, then you need to reassign your roles for that condition so that everything is covered and you are not missing out priorities. As a team you need to give yourself some time to upskill, become experts and evolve into the sailors you need to be, so give the team the time and space to do this.

© Thom Touw

What To Do If You Can't Hold Your Lane?

There will be some days where you have just got your set-up wrong. Hopefully this doesn't have to be the end of your race: stay neutral and try to problem solve. Firstly, systematically work through all the active settings you have: jib car, jibsheet, for the crew; the mainsail set-up for the helm. Have you just got yourself out of whack on a few things, especially if there has been a condition change since you tuned pre-race?

Try to articulate to each other the feeling of why you are slow: that can help identify the problem. Does it feel sticky and that you are not accelerating on the gusts? Do you just feel underpowered? It could just be a very subtle change in conditions means that a different technique is required.

So, check in with where you are on that. Are you flat? Or too heeled to windward or leeward? Has the chop steepened and would crew weight further apart to stop see-sawing be better? Look at your competitors and see who is doing a better job: can you copy them?

From a racing perspective you need to take a deep breath and accept that things are not going to be perfect. Continually getting bounced on to the wrong shift or holding on until you have a perfect lane will get you more out of sync with the fleet and more on the back foot. I'm not going to pretend there is a magic system that will make this problem go away but it's important not to give up.

The Next Leg

In the final quarter of the upwind it's good to remind yourselves of the course you are doing: if trapezoid, is it a hoist on to a reach or downwind?

If you are hoisting onto a downwind leg:
- Remind yourself of any tidal situation or major windshift that might be creating a long tack for the downwind.
- What position are you rounding the mark in and what opportunities might that create? Would you be looking to gybe before the pack of boats ahead so wanting to execute a low hoist so you don't get stuck above people. Or is there a pack of boats behind so you need to hoist high to defend?

If you are hoisting onto a reach:
- Start trying to get a visual on the reach mark and figure out if your reach is tight or broad.
- Is there tide or a shift making it tighter or broader?
- Where is the opportunity? By going high, or a low hoist?

A lot of opportunity is created in the first 2 seconds of boat positioning in a hoist. As others have their heads down in the boat it is a great moment to pounce. It will depend on whether strategically there is an opportunity there, but how you set up on your layline approach will hugely influence being able to execute it. For example, it will be hard to execute a gybe set onto the downwind if you over-stand on the starboard layline and a boat tacks inside of you as you approach the mark. Likewise, if the reach is really tight, being made tighter by tide, tacking in late at the windward mark under a bunch of starboard tackers will make your reach difficult. So, the type of hoist you will ideally execute will influence the final part of your windward mark approach. There is always flexibility in this and good boat handling in any situation can open an opportunity that didn't seem to be there.

CHAPTER 16
Downwind

The Hoist

As discussed at the end of the last chapter, the hoist is crucial in positioning yourself for some overtaking opportunities on the downwind leg.

Ideally your communication on the final part of the beat will have determined the style of hoist you are looking for and the hoist is the moment to zone in to an internal focus and execute some boat handling effectively and efficiently.

As soon as the kite is set you need to feed back to your helm if you feel you need to go high and fast or low and slow (see the section on downwind in the Straight-Line Speed chapter: p94).

Helping Your Helm

Although your main priority is speed, as an output from your team roles' discussion, there might be input that you can give from a tactical and strategic perspective too. In my limited experience downwind tactics can be a pretty lonely place for the helm, so some questions that help them formulate the plan could work:

- What's going on?
- Have you got the leeward marks?
- Where have the gains and losses been?

You might be totally happy to know nothing until you turn the corner for the upwind, but that information could be really valuable in your second beat strategy.

The Next Leg

Before you get to the drop, discuss which leeward mark you will round (if it is a gate) and which way you think will be favoured up the next beat. What did you learn up the previous beat(s) that might influence your strategy on the next beat? Have the conditions changed: wind direction, speed and tide?

Beware that the call on leeward marks can be changed due to other boats, so be prepared to change your process.

The Drop

After the excitement of some close racing downwind it's really easy to get distracted from the process of the drop, especially if you need to pull off some tight boat handling in a congested area. Again it's one of those moments that you need to zone out of the noise and execute your role quickly and accurately. Don't let shouting from other boats or your own boat slow you down.

Depending on what tactical scenario you are in there will be a whole load of possible boat handling manoeuvres to do. In training sessions with other boats I'd really encourage aggressively attacking each other all the way into the leeward marks so that your boat handling gets pressured and sharp and your eyes are opened to the possibilities that work, could work and absolutely don't work. The leeward mark is definitely an area where you can get distracted and might win the battle on an individual boat but lose the war on the rest of the fleet.

The Hoist

A lot of times there will be little tactical opportunity on the reach and it turns into a bit of a procession. But you need to keep alert to the opportunities there might be, especially on the hoist.

As a general rule, people stay high out of the windward mark and hoist once the boat in front has committed to the hoist. Would a low hoist work with where you are in the fleet? Would over-standing slightly on the starboard layline get you above all the layline congestion? You could then just hoist above it and sail around the congestion.

The gain from a low hoist might not be realised until the final 50 metres of the reach, as that is when you can finally sail higher and faster and the boats in the procession will finally sail to the mark on a lower, slower angle, so you will pop through their dirty air with speed.

Speed & Communication

Obviously, on the reach, the spinnaker is your main priority because if it collapses and you are in a tight lane, it can be misery as the whole fleet passes you.

The wind that is coming to you is perfectly in your line of sight and this also means that you are totally prepared for it in terms of leverage. If it's a big lull, make sure that you have enough space on your trapeze wire to get in far enough and quickly enough as rolling to windward on a reach is a nightmare. It could be that taking your weight in your front hand, unhooking and swinging your weight into the boat could save you from a really big lull in pressure.

You need to provide feedback on the line of the boats behind you and what they are doing. Although this is looking away from your spinnaker, if the boats are going high, the helm has quite a lot on to change set-up and to match them, so needs the crew for that input.

You will also know through your spinnaker trimming how much 'range' you have left to sheet in the spinnaker and go higher if necessary. So, if you need height tactically or strategically, call to your helm that you have some room on the sheeting for more height.

Practise what the speed and angle of sailing fast on a reach feels like. There might be times where you are holding high to defend a group from behind and actually you don't need to, if you just drop the bow a few degrees you will just sail away from them in the right direction to the mark and they will be nowhere near for an attack.

Like the downwind, the reach will be a series of different techniques linked in together, as the pressure increases and decreases. For a load of different reasons, most reaches I have sailed in my racing career have always ended with a slightly slow, low mode at the end so always using the opportunities to sail low and fast when you can will equal metres gained at the end of the reach.

Tight Reaches

You can go around the windward mark and due to a left windshift, too much wind or the mark being set too high, the call will be not to hoist. If it looks like it will never be a spinnaker leg, then sail the shortest distance to the mark and, if you have an adjustable car system for the jib, pull them max forward so the top of your jib works down the reach. (BUT REMEMBER you've done this and to put them back to upwind position on the downwind).

However, if it looks like it's only a few degrees off and holding high for a section of the leg would then give you enough height to hoist, then hold high and sail a fast 2-sail reach until you think you can hoist and make the reach mark.

I haven't got a great rule for the judgement call on when to hoist, it's practice and experience. Remember that if it's windy you will lose some height during the hoist. If you haven't hoisted out of the mark you invariably get involved in a bit of a waiting game with your competitors around you, about who will pull the trigger first. It feels hard to jump the queue on the hoist, so the tendency is always to wait until the person in front has gone for it but, if you think they are over-standing, go for it and race for the hoist. If the boat in front of you matches you straightaway, you are no better or worse off regarding them. If they delay a bit, they immediately put themselves in a really difficult situation as you will be back on angle and sailing fast a few boat lengths below their line, which will be a nightmare for them as, when they want to bear away and hoist, you will be there.

If you've hoisted the spinnaker and you are not making it, don't panic! If you've still got a significant amount of distance to sail, then lots can still happen: you might get a lull or a shift back right and end up making it easily. If hoisting was just the wrong decision and you are going to end up sailing with the spinnaker flapping for a good portion of the reach, then just suck up the loss and drop it early. Otherwise, hold on to it as long as you can, until you are on a fast, tight reach angle and then the helm can blow the kite halyard and it will flap from the top for the remaining bit of the leg. Pull the sheet in tight to stop any twists getting in the kite. As the helm blows the kite be ready for the massive depower.

End Of The Leg

Towards the end of the first reach, locate the leeward marks and discuss any strategic decisions that would be relevant, similar to your windward mark approach if you were bearing away straight onto a downwind. As you have sailed a reasonable distance on the top reach and you are effectively in a new section of water that you've not raced in before consider a few of the wider strategic options that you discussed pre start, are you closer to any land that will affect the wind or waves?

If you are racing a triangle, at the end of the second reach, talk about the next beat as discussed at the end of the downwind leg (p116).

© Thom Touw

BRINGING IT ALL TOGETHER

© Thom Touw

PART 4

CHAPTER 18

Being The Best Crew

There will be loads of reasons why you started sailing and why you are good at it, and those will be important factors in being part of a great team. How you blend and grow the individual skills of each player into being a team together will ultimately make you repeatedly successful.

This is my take on what I think makes the difference on being good and being awesome.

Firstly, I can't recommend enough trying to seek out and talk to people that have been there and done it or have some experience in the path you are trying to follow. Everyone will have their lessons, why they succeeded and why they failed. Added to your own experience, it will fast track your route to the top. You don't have to follow their advice, but it's always good to listen with an open mind. Sometimes the fact that you categorically disagree with their opinion could spur you into action along your winning path.

Secondly, ask for help along the way. When you move up from youth to senior sailing there is this will to prove that you can do it on your own and be your own person, but let people help you, give yourself and your team time and room to make

mistakes and learn from them.

If you are new to crewing and particularly if you are transitioning from being a helm, fully embrace what that means you need to change and adapt both physically, mentally and around the course.

Fitness & Strength

Different boats will have different demands, with a really obvious starting point of whether you are sailing a trapezing or hiking boat.

If you are totally serious about your sailing, get some expert advice on how to tailor a programme for you. If you can't find a sailing-specific expert, explain as much as possible to a mainstream fitness coach: what your physical role in the boat is and where you need to improve. Be as specific as possible outside the boat as it will have the biggest impact in the boat.

The internet is a great resource for finding all sorts of specific programmes; follow your favourite athletes on Strava or Instagram and see what fitness programmes they are doing. If you are trying to build a fitness programme yourself it's worth getting some expert advice so you perform the exercises with good form.

As a starting point:
- **Hiking crew**: Focus on building strength and endurance in your legs, abdominals and back.
- **Trapezing crew**: Abdominals, back and shoulders.

Spend time on some agility training because fast foot and hand speed is useful to everyone, especially as a crew. It's totally trainable and you'll notice rapid improvements.

© Thom Touw

CHAPTER 19
Being A Great Team

It is my very firm opinion that for a two-person sailing team to achieve their absolute potential, both parts of that team need to be operating at maximum capacity. There will be times when this ebbs and flows, but I think you can only win a gold medal if you have an environment that promotes that and empowers each team member to be the best they can be.

That will look totally different for every team you observe but, if you want to achieve your potential, invest some time and energy into understanding what you individually need to be the best version of yourself, share this with your team-mate and discuss how you can bring it together to be greater than the sum of your parts.

What is the environment that you respond well in? Is it calm and relaxed or do you need some pressure to get you going? Do you enjoy relentlessly committing hours doing stuff, or do you need to sit and reflect on things to be better?

Everyone will be different and at different phases in your campaign you'll need to be flexible on your approach, but it is good to know about yourself and your team-mate's preferred modes of operating and agree what your go-to method is as a team.

Communicating

There is so much going on around a race course and it is changing all the time. But simply, most observations that we are making judgements on are factual, so in an environment with no stress and no time pressure we would have a great success rate at making the right decision. Why does it seem so much harder on a race course?

How we communicate that information around the boat will dramatically influence how successfully it is executed.

The first vital cornerstone of good communication is having the same language. Spend time onshore talking through the race and figuring out what your team means when 'the fleet are all with us' or 'bow down to push forward' and so on. Come up with set pieces or code words, which cut down on the need for words in tight situations, like the start or mark roundings.

If you are struggling with this and feel like you are continually at odds with what is being said and what is being heard, consider recording yourselves around a race course and analysing it later.

The output from the discussion of your upwind roles should have created the framework for your priorities around observation for a given sailing condition and who in the team is communicating them. Be strict with each other on this so that you begin to build and consistently execute a system. As you get better and have more bandwidth, the system can evolve and develop into something more specific and can play to your team's strengths and weaknesses.

Accepting the areas where you individually need help is no bad thing. Firstly, it just highlights what you need to get better at but secondly, if your helm is really good at them, then it might be something you don't need to bother about. Hannah was really good at laylines, I was quite happy for her to take them on!

Emotional Control

Emotional control gets talked about a lot in sport. Understanding what it meant for me was the biggest single breakthrough in my career and essentially opened up a whole world of potential.

If you are racing to get selected for a team, win a medal or an outright win, emotions are involved. The results sheet can be a lonely place: we see it as a reflection of our talent, of how much effort we are putting in. It can be frustrating or exhilarating and has all the potential to be distracting whether things are going well or badly.

On a race course that internal conversation is adding bias to concrete facts and swaying the outcome of your decision. When you are in a team of two or more, it's not just your own inner dialogue to process: team-mates can throw in their emotion and further cloud your judgement of facts. Silencing this chat, both internally and between yourselves, will give you brain space and clarity to keep observing clearly, identifying the facts, analysing them, prioritising and making the right decisions.

If things go wrong, it's back to observing, analysing, prioritising and executing and the same if things go right. In the heat of a race, blame for mistakes doesn't help this process. A 'no blame team' doesn't absolve anyone of any responsibility for making the right observations and hopefully decisions and, if roles get neglected and mistakes get made, someone is accountable, and you go back to the process of building your method.

Our assumption was always that everyone is trying their best for the team and not attempting to sabotage it from the inside. I understand that there are days when it doesn't feel like that!! But give everyone a break; let people make mistakes and build their experience, analyse what got missed and how to not make that mistake again. If the mistake gets made again, analyse why and change your process.

Getting angry and emotional about these things in the moment (whether it be internally, externally, as the person responsible for the mistake or not)

distracts everyone from making the next right observation and decision and when things have gone wrong that is the absolute priority.

It's hard to never respond emotionally to things both on and off the water and it's important to work through things that might be causing you frustration, so understanding how you and your team-mates emotionally respond to situations is important. People deal with things in different ways, some people go into their shells and withdraw, others shout and rant: both can be damaging to the team and performance. Something that might help you get back in the present could send your team-mate backwards, so I'd encourage talking this through as a team, honestly discussing how you impact on each other and figure out the best way forwards.

Planning

Campaigns are successful because of the planning and detail. It sounds boring but, unfortunately, it's true! Whether you are planning an Olympic campaign or want to sail locally, a bit of thought can make it more successful and enjoyable.

Firstly, there is the obvious logistical planning that needs to get done. Whether you are sailing at your club, travelling the country or the world, timings need to be agreed and stuff needs to get booked and paid for. Some people love this stuff and others hate it so, if you can play to your individual strengths within the team, then that's great. If you all hate it, simply write a job list and allocate it out fairly. Include all the aspects from logistics and accommodation, to boat work, making spares, on the water food and drink. This side of sailing can be hugely time consuming; decide as a team how important it is to you and how much time you'll allocate to it.

If you are campaigning to get better, I would recommend time spent sitting down, evaluating past performances, finding areas of weakness and coming up with a process to improve. There are a number of ways to do this goal-setting process and different methods will appeal to different personalities. My biggest advice on this is that the method doesn't matter – but choose a way that means something to all of you in the team and doesn't take too much time otherwise you'll only do it once a year. The easier your process, the more frequently you'll check in and 'plan, do, review' and your team will constantly be progressing. A method that kept me really engaged with this process was that we tailored the skills we needed to be good at specifically to our outcome venues and regattas.

There are a number of different techniques but essentially you need to identify where there are improvements to be made and then come up with a process for doing that. This can be done as a team, but it can be really useful to use a third party as a question master: to help you see where your blind spots are and get to the bottom of problems. Often this perspective from the outside will make you see things differently.

Use this information to focus your training, improve your weak areas and, importantly, maintain your strengths. Don't switch off this learning attitude through a regatta, there is still the day, weekend or week to understand the problem, change technique and do it better.

To Close

Firstly, I'm hopeful that there have been some useful things in this book to improve your sailing and racing performance and your enjoyment of our amazing sport. But secondly, understand that there is rarely an absolute right or only way to achieve something and, with some good communication and teamwork, most obstacles can be overcome.

I look forward to seeing you out on the water!

© Thom Touw

GLOSSARY

Apparent wind	The wind experienced by a moving boat, made up of the true wind & the wind generated by the boat's movement
Asymmetric	Boat with a downwind sail (spinnaker) with a fixed luff
Back	Jib held on windward side to help the boat bear away
Batten	Strip put in a sail to stiffen its leech
Beam reach	Point of sailing with the wind directly abeam
Bear away	Changing course away from the wind
Bear away set	Hoisting and setting the spinnaker while bearing away
Beat	Close-hauled course to windward, involving tacking
Bight	An open loop in a rope
Block	A pulley
Boom	Horizontal spar attached to the foot of the mainsail
Bow	Front part of a boat
Bowline	Knot used to tie a loop in the end of a rope
Bowsprit	Spar that extends forward from the bow to support an asymmetric spinnaker
Broad reach	Point of sail when the wind is behind the beam
Capsize	Point when the mast touches the water
Centreboard case	Case in which the centreboard is held in the cockpit
Cleat	Fitting to lock rope in place & hold it under tension
Clew	Lower aft corner of a sail
Close-hauled	Point of sailing closest to the wind
Close reach	Point of sailing midway between close-hauled and a beam reach
Cockpit	Area in a boat surrounded by the deck where sailors sit
Cover	Positioning yourself to windward of another boat
Committee boat	Official boat which racing is run from
Cunningham	Rope which attaches to the tack of a sail to pull it down
Current	A flow of water
Deck	Top surface of a boat
Dirty wind	Disturbed wind caused by other boats to windward
Downhaul	Rope attached to a spinnaker to pull it into the chute / Control line to lower the height of the spinnaker pole or stop it going in the air
Downwind	Sailing in the same direction as the wind / away from the wind
Drop	Lowering the spinnaker (or other sail)
Ease	Slacken or let a rope out
Fairlead	Fitting rope runs through
Flatten	To bring the boat horizontal from heeled
Foils	Collective term used for centreboard and rudder
Foot	Bottom edge of a sail / to sail further off the wind
Footloop	Loop on gunwale for someone trapezing to put their foot into for stability
Foredeck	Deck in front of the mast

Forestay	Forward stay supporting the mast to which the jib is attached
Goose-winged	Sailing downwind with the jib the opposite side to the mainsail
Gunwale	Edge between the hull and the deck
Guy	See spinnaker guy
Gybe	To turn the boat so the stern passes through the wind
Gybe set	Hoisting and setting the spinnaker during / immediately after a gybe
Halyard	Rope or wire used to hoist the sails
Head	Top corner of a sail
Head to wind	Boat facing directly into the wind
Head up	Changing course towards the wind
Heel	Angle of the boat to windward or leeward from horizontal
Hiking	To lean out to counter the heeling force of the wind
Hoist	Raising the spinnaker (or other sail)
Jib car	Moveable fairlead for the jibsheet
Jib cleat	Cleat used to hold the jibsheet under tension
Jib stick	Pole used to goose-wing the jib
Jibsheet	Rope to control the set of the jib
Kicking strap / kicker	Purchase system to hold the boom down
Kinetics	Using sudden body movements to help power the boat (e.g. bouncing)
Kite	See spinnaker
Lane	Course which keeps you away from the effect of other boats
Lazy sheet	Jib or spinnaker sheet to windward which is not being used to control the sail on that tack
Lee / Leeward	The side away from the wind
Lee bow	Sailing to leeward of a boat & giving them dirty wind
Leech	Aft edge of a sail
Luff	Leading edge of a sail
Mast	Vertical spar extending up from the boat to which sails & rigging attach
One-design	Class of boat where all the boats are to the same design
Overlap	When any part of a boat is beside another / when a sail is beside another
Pitchpoling	Capsizing end over end
Planing	When a boat lifts its bows out of the water & reduces its drag
Port	Left-hand side of a boat
Pump	Pull in a sail rapidly
Rack	Lateral extension to the hull on some boats
Rack tube	The tubes around the rack
Reach	Point of sail when the wind is abeam
Rig	General term for mast, stays and sails
Roll gybe	Using body weight to speed the process of gybing
Roll tack	Using body weight to speed the process of tacking
Rounding	Turning around a racing mark
Rule 42	A rule which limits the amount of body movement to help propel the boat
Run	Point of sail going away from the wind
Sea breeze	An onshore wind generated by temperature difference between land & sea
Sheave	The wheel within a block

Sheet	Rope to control the set of a sail
Shock cord	Elastic rope
Shroud	Wire supporting the side of the mast
Side deck	Deck either side of the cockpit
Skiff	Fairly flat planing dinghy
Slot	Gap between the jib & the mainsail
Soak	Sailing as far off the wind as possible while still maintaining VMG
Spinnaker	Parachute-like downwind sail
Spinnaker bag	Bag at the front of the cockpit in which the spinnaker is stored when not in use
Spinnaker chute	Tube from bow to cockpit into which the spinnaker is lowered & stored
Spinnaker guy	The sheet attached to the windward clew of the spinnaker
Spinnaker pole	Spar to set the spinnaker from
Spinnaker sheet	Rope to control the set of the spinnaker
Spreader	Strut to deflect the shrouds & control the bending characteristics of the mast
Spreader mark	Offset mark at the start of the downwind leg to prevent those rounding the windward mark heading downwind immediately
Starboard	Right-hand side of a boat
Stay	See shroud
Stern	Back part of a boat
Symmetric	Boat with a downwind sail (spinnaker) which is symmetrical
Tack	Lower forward corner of a sail / To turn the boat so the bow passes through the wind
Telltale	Strip of wool or fabric attached to a sail to indicate airflow over the sail
Thwart	Lateral seat amidships of the cockpit
Toestrap	Strip of webbing running fore and aft for feet to be hooked under when hiking
Transit	A line going through two fixed points
Transom	Aft surface of a boat
Trapeze	Device attached to the mast to allow the whole body to be extended outboard to counter the heeling force of the wind
Trapeze harness	Harness with a hook which the sailor wears to use the trapeze
Trapeze hook	Hook on the trapeze harness which attached to the trapeze wire
Trapeze wire	Wire from the mast which the sailor hooks on to
Traveller	Fitting or rope to adjust the position of the mainsheet
Trigger pull	Accelerating the boat at the start
Trim	Adjusting the setting of a sail / The fore-aft angle of the boat
Tuning	Adjusting the rig settings to maximise speed
Twinner	Rope with a fairlead attached to the spinnaker sheet to allow its angle to be controlled
Unweight	Take the weight off
Uphaul	Control line to raise the height of the spinnaker pole
Upwind	Sailing closer to the wind than a beam reach / towards the wind
Vang	See kicking strap
VMG	Velocity made good: the speed of travelling towards the chosen destination
Windward	The side towards the wind
Wire-to-wire	Going directly from trapezing on one side to the other in a tack

FERNHURST
BOOKS

We hope you enjoyed this book

If you did, **please post a review on Amazon**

Discover more books on

SAILING · RACING · CRUISING · MOTOR BOATING

SWIMMING · DIVING · SURFING

CANOEING · KAYAKING · FISHING

View our full range of titles at **www.fernhurstbooks.com**

Sign up to receive details of new books & exclusive special offers at
www.fernhurstbooks.com/register

Get to know us more on **social media**

THE ANDREW SIMPSON
SAILING FOUNDATION

The charity was founded to honour the life and legacy of Andrew 'Bart' Simpson MBE, Olympic Gold & Silver medalist and America's Cup Sailor by using sailing to improve the lives of young people.

Working with sailing providers internationally, the Foundation offers the challenges of a sailing environment to promote health and wellbeing, and to develop personal skills that will improve a young person's ability to succeed in life.

SUPPORT US

info@andrewsimpsonsailing.org
andrewsimpsonfoundation.org

@AndrewSimpsonSa Andrew Simpson Sailing Foundation
andrewsimpsonsailingfoundation sailonbart

ANDREW SIMPSON SAILING FOUNDATION